Cosmic Satire in the Contemporary Novel

Cosmic Satire
in the
Contemporary Novel

John W. Tilton

LEWISBURG
BUCKNELL UNIVERSITY PRESS
LONDON: ASSOCIATED UNIVERSITY PRESSES

Associated University Presses, Inc.
Cranbury, New Jersey 08512

Associated University Presses
Magdalen House
136–148 Tooley Street
London SE1 2TT, England

Library of Congress Cataloging in Publication Data

Tilton, John Wightman, 1928-
　　Cosmic satire in the contemporary novel.

　　Bibliography: p.
　　Includes index.
　　1. American fiction—20th century—History and criticism.　2. Satire,
American—History and criticism.　3. Wilson, John Anthony Burgess,
1917-　　　. A clockwork orange. I. Title.
PS379.T5　813'.03　　　75-18240
ISBN 0-8387-1378-5

For Bill Koehler, Steve Meilleur, and Jack Lowry, a special few of the many students who—to paraphrase John Barth—responded to my heartfelt ineptitude, endured my heartless skill, and thereby inspired in me as much of that rare combination as I am capable of—passionate virtuosity.

With grateful acknowledgment of valuable assistance from Dennis Baumwoll, a critic of extraordinary acumen and generosity, and from Mildred Martin, who offered encouragement and help when needed most, as she has often done in our long and cherished association.

CONTENTS

ACKNOWLEDGMENTS

Grateful acknowledgment is made for permission to reprint the following material:

Reprinted from *A Clockwork Orange* by Anthony Burgess, by permission of W. W. Norton & Company, Inc. Copyright © 1962 by Anthony Burgess. Copyright © 1963 by W. W. Norton & Company, Inc., and of Deborah Rogers Ltd.

Reprinted from *Giles Goat-Boy*, copyright © 1966 by John Barth. Reprinted by permission of Doubleday & Co., Inc. Permission granted by the author's agent, Lurton Blassingame. Copyright © 1966 by John Barth.

Reprinted from *Slaughterhouse-Five*, copyright © 1969 by Kurt Vonnegut, Jr. Reprinted by permission of Delacorte Press/ Seymour Lawrence.

The chapter on *Giles Goat-Boy* is reprinted, in a revised form, from *Bucknell Review* 18, no. 1. Copyright © 1970 by *Bucknell Review*.

Cosmic Satire
in the
Contemporary Novel

The unflinching eye detects, the intellect names, the heart goes out in compassion; and the life-force of every life-loving heart will be finally tested, challenged, and measured by its capacity to regard with such compassion whatever has been by the eye perceived and by the intellect named.

Joseph Campbell, *Myths to Live By*

1

ON LEARNING
BY GOING WHERE THE CRITIC
HAS TO GO

In scope and length, this critical study of contemporary satiric fiction is a modest undertaking. It is devoted to only three novels, though one of them—John Barth's *Giles Goat-Boy*—is a challenging 710 pages of scatological fun and games escalated to heights of mythopoeic complexity and satiric-philosophic profundity the likes of which will not be seen again for a long time. But I do have a few immodest intentions, the chief being to show that the much shorter and apparently less complex *A Clockwork Orange* and *Slaughterhouse-Five* are on their own terms equally as challenging as *Giles Goat-Boy*. Because of this and its other aims, I like to think that it is the kind of book that *has* to be written on contemporary satiric fiction.

Let me try to suggest briefly why I believe that these three novels demand the approach I have taken. Then, under the heading of, "This Shaking Keeps One Steady: Cosmic Satire," I shall sketch my reasons for dealing with them collectively, in spite of their obvious differences in content and form.

THINKING BY FEELING: THE CRITICAL APPROACH

First, I need the reader's assent to three simple premises that inhere in the terms *contemporary, satiric,* and *fiction.* Novels published in 1962, 1966, and 1969 are indisputably contemporary, since that term embraces all literature of the past twenty years or so. But since the term *contemporary* has no distinct substantial meaning, it can not be applied indiscriminately on the basis of dates alone. To give it substance, one must delimit the immense variety of contemporary literature and isolate the qualities that give each work its distinctive contemporaneity. Only by avoiding easy generalizations and by inducing from each individual work its inherent concern with aspects of life in the present time can one arrive at a meaningful definition of "contemporary" and proceed from there to determine whether other works bear enough resemblance to be usefully classified according to that definition. Generalizations must evolve from, not be arbitrarily imposed upon, the bewildering variety of current literature.

To expect the reader to grant that these three novels are undeniably satiric without first defining or offering a theory of contemporary satire may be asking a bit much; but ask it I must, for my premise is that the major obstacle to a true perception and sound evaluation of the satiric is a rigid preconception of what satire is or ought to be. To the extent that Burgess, Barth, and Vonnegut are conventional social satirists—and, to be sure, as shall be seen, they are perceptive observers of the contemporary social scene and highly skilled practitioners of the techniques of satirical attack—one's acquaintance with satiric literature of the past and with satiric criticism and theory should enable one to discern the tone and manner of satire and to recognize its techniques and objects. But the problem is that no theory of conventional or traditional satire, based as it must be upon past satirical practice, can possibly embrace the contemporaneity of their satire. To grasp the distinctive satiric character of a contemporary novel and ultimately to formulate a theory of satire that adequately describes the novelist's actual practice, the reader must respond sensitively to what the satirist is doing and saying in the specific work at hand. Satire is and ought to be what the creative satirist makes it become.

I hope I have been consistent enough to enable one to anticipate the third premise: the fictions of Burgess, Barth, and Vonnegut are highly imaginative narrative forms, employing novelistic techniques both conventional and innovative; they therefore invite, indeed demand, the most sophisticated and comprehensive analysis that the professional critic of the novel can bring to bear. And the chief measure of this sophistication is his receptivity to new departures and his ability to respond to the unique complexities of the form that each novelist has evolved.

In seeking assent to these premises, I have really begun to describe a very special critical approach to contemporary satiric fiction, one that demands not just a sensitive and alert response to the apparently distinct constituents of each work but also a recognition of the organic inter-dependence of all of the constituents. Though difficult to define, the genre in which Burgess, Barth, and Vonnegut wrote can not be ap-proached simply as long prose fiction in manner and intent satiric on subjects of contemporary relevance. To put the matter negatively for a moment, the critic who attempts to isolate, describe, and evaluate either the novelistic techniques and formal structures of these works, or their satiric techniques and objects, or their commentary on contemporary issues will inevitably produce a distortion because he will have violated the organic interdependence of all three of the constituents.

For example, a reviewer of *Slaughterhouse-Five* comments that the scene of Billy Pilgrim's watching war movies backwards is "as effective as any short passage ever written against war,"[1] an observation that can be made only if one ignores the complex narrative context of the scene: the satire is not directed against war but against the Billy Pilgrims of this world who can not face the reality of wars, escape into a fantasy world, and thus deny the significance of the lives lost in wars that Vonnegut knows will never cease. One can readily discount a review of the novel, but when responsible academic critics produce an intensive study like *The Vonnegut Statement*[2] that suffers from a similar single-mindedness, one so simplistic in its approach to Vonnegut that it interprets *Slaughterhouse-Five* without awareness of its satiric components and praises Vonnegut for having created in Billy Pilgrim a "transcendent hero," I for one am distressed.

Another illustration is provided by the critic of *A Clockwork Orange* who asserts that Burgess's

adroit shock tactics with plot and language, expertise with satire, and partiality to apocalypse—all enviable attributes and potential pluses normally—come dangerously close here to out flanking the substantive ideas. Done as these novels [*The Wanting Seed* and *A Clockwork Orange*] are, with immense energy and cleverness, their sheer "physicalness" all but crushes their metaphysics.[3]

Behind the apparent blatancy of this separation of ideas, novelistic techniques, and satire lies a fundamental deficiency in critical approach, a failure to respond creatively to the interdependence of all three. Without assimilating that "physicalness," the critic can not respond sensibly to either the novelistic techniques or the satirical and as a consequence can never determine what the "substantive ideas" or the "metaphysics" of the novel are or, for that matter, whether Burgess's commentary on contemporary issues emerges as an isolable idea-content at all.

Unfortunately, in illustrating the need for a critical approach that will allow one to read these novels as highly complex organic wholes, I have indulged in polemics. I hasten to say that I have no intention of engaging any further in polemic criticism: rebuttal is tiresome and self-serving, smacking as it does of the unpleasant one-upmanship practiced ad infinitum by academic critics. If my critical approach has merit, only the chapters to follow can show it. Those chapters will take one inside the novels where I had to go, feeling my way around and responding as my critical instincts suggested until I realized what the novels demanded of me.

I emerged with the convictions that I have been illustrating: that these novelists both employ and depart from conventional novelistic techniques and create new forms in order to convey a distinctive satiric perspective; that their satiric intentions are fulfilled by means of conventional satiric techniques that the satirist-novelist has transformed by fusing them with innovative novelistic techniques; and that he has had to do so in order to reflect the complexity and ambiguity of contemporary issues in which he, as a participant in the human predicament, has a vitally personal involvement.

In recognition of this configuration of the satiric-fictional practice of Burgess, Barth, and Vonnegut, I suggest that their novels yield their true import and reveal their artistic value only to the critic willing to yield himself to them, without imposing rigid generic preconceptions or expectations derived from the history and theory of either the novel or of satire and without bringing to them preconceived normative judgments about the stance an artist should take on contemporary issues, yet with all of his critical faculties alert and his knowledge of the novel, of satire, and of the conditions of contemporary life in readiness to help him respond creatively to the unique work at hand.

Frankly, I can not judge whether in my reading of Burgess, Barth, and Vonnegut I have lived up to this critical credo. But I have tried to meet the demands they have made on me. This study, then, is an invitation to join me on the inside to see whether everyone will agree on those demands and the proper responses to them.

THIS SHAKING KEEPS ONE STEADY: COSMIC SATIRE

For me, the attempt to meet the demands of these three novels has resulted in a growing awareness that they involve the reader in a distinctly powerful contemporary satire that yet has striking correspondences to the most compelling satires of the past, *Gulliver's Travels*, for instance. In words that Swift himself might well have spoken of his parodic satire of travel literature and the *voyage imaginaire*, John Barth provides in his comment on *Giles Goat-Boy* one of my reasons for calling this kind of satire "cosmic":

> My intention was to begin by satirizing the basic myth [of the wandering hero] and then, hopefully, escalate the satire into something larger, darker, and more compassionate.[4]

Each in his own way, Barth, Burgess, and Vonnegut have escalated what might have been mere parody or social satire to achieve that "something larger, darker, and more compassionate," as Swift did.

Each of the novels demonstrably originates in an identifiable contemporary milieu; and the clerkish critic of satire can readily fill his notebook with lists of specific people, institutions, events, situations, and issues that stimulated the initial satiric impulse. And the more imaginative critic can readily see that these specifics are representative of conditions that obtain beyond the satirist's immediately observable milieu. But cosmic pounds itself. Compassion is the attitude of cosmic satire, compassion because the satirist well understands the need for illusion in a mad world, compassion because he can not be superior to or detached from a plight that he himself participates in. I believe that a great deal of the moving power that cosmic satire generates, the aesthetic power of these novels, whose structural tension engages the reader's deepest emotions, emanates from the artist's honest confrontation with his own dilemma: attracted to the illusory himself, he can resist the temptation to deform reality only by constantly reaffirming his tenuous belief in the value of his individuality and integrity that he knows he would lose were he to succumb to the attraction of illusion. Conceiving of illusion as a symptom of insanity, the cosmic satirists need to struggle to maintain their sanity. In cosmic satire one always feels the presence of artists who make the reader feel and share their hope for continued sanity and their troubled and troubling awareness that a moment's weakness or a twist of fate can destroy the psychic tension on which sanity depends—and cast them among the benighted creatures. To paraphrase Roethke's "The Waking," this tension makes for the shaking that keeps them—and everyone else—steady.

"Self-knowledge is always bad news," says Max Spielman in *Giles Goat-Boy*. True. If the chapters to follow succeed in their intention, one can then agree as well that contemporary satiric fiction showing the lengths one goes to avoid that bad news is, aesthetically, very good news indeed.

NOTES

1. *Time*, 11 April 1969, p. 106.
2. Jerome Klinkowitz and John Somer, eds., *The Vonnegut Statement* (New York: Dell Publishing Co., 1973).
3. Robert K. Morris, *The Consolations of Ambiguity* (Columbia, Missouri: University of Missouri Press, 1971), p. 58.
4. Quoted by Phyllis Meras, "John Barth: A Truffle No Longer," New York *Times*, 7 August 1966, sec. 7, p. 22.
5. (New York: Dell Publishing Co., 1969), p. 140.
6. "Against Dryness," *Encounter* 16 (January 1961):20.
7. Ibid.

2

A CLOCKWORK ORANGE: AWARENESS IS ALL

Anthony Burgess says that Stanley Kubrick was not aware of the existence of the last chapter of *A Clockwork Orange*, the seventh chapter of part three, until he was well under way with the production of his film version.[1] No wonder: the American edition, published by W. W. Norton and Company in 1963, contains no word whatsoever to inform its readers that the last chapter has been deleted; and it was then and is to this day the only edition readily available to American readers. Though Burgess may be at fault for acceding to Norton's ultimatum—agree to drop the last chapter or we will not publish—I can not blame him anymore than I can John Barth for acquiescing to an editorial demand for a changed ending to *The Floating Opera* to have that first novel published. Prick an impecunious novelist and he bleeds.

Barth's worth as a writer gradually won him enough clout to have *The Floating Opera* republished with the ending he originally wrote. Ironically, it was evidently the popularity of the Kubrick film that gradually led some interested American readers to discover that the British edition contains the ending Burgess originally wrote. But short of ordering a copy of the complete novel from Heinemann in London, Americans must do without the last chapter. To compound the irony, many English readers will now join American readers in ignorance of the complete

21

novel: the publisher of the English paperback edition has deleted the last chapter to make the novel conform to the film.

There is a point to this prefatory note on the publishing history of *A Clockwork Orange*: I am going to comment on the complete novel, even though I realize that, a few aficionados aside, the world may never have the chance to read it. As a critic I have no choice, not only because I feel bound to honor the writer's intentions and to resist the commercialism of publishing houses but also because a critic of *A Clockwork Orange* would be derelict if he did not consult the original novel and at least describe the differences in technique, form, and impact between it and the "edited" novel. I also believe that the shortening of the novel constitutes a gross truncation, that the "edited" version is a considerably lesser work. My analysis of the technical-satiric patterns of the complete novel constitutes a low-keyed argument that the complete novel is superior to the truncated version. Ultimately, of course, each reader will have to decide for himself whether the deletion of the last chapter makes for a gain or a loss.

The major contention of my argument—fair warning—is that the last chapter makes of *A Clockwork Orange* a better novel than Burgess may realize he has written. Perhaps without perfect sincerity, Burgess has recently said that he does not like the novel because it preaches too much and entertains too little. Certainly if one accepts his statements, one would have to share his evaluation. Describing social conditions in the England of 1959-60, Burgess informs of proposals actually made to employ conditioning techniques to rid England of the evils of the Teddy Boys and the Mods and Rockers. He comments:

> My own horror, my own rage, during the final year of these proposals, I see now, was very much the rage of a Lancashire Catholic, some-body who had been brought up on the notion of the primacy of the human will, somebody who had been always taught to believe that men have the power of choice . . . . And I felt and I knew and I still know that once the power of choice is removed from the human soul then that human soul ceases to be human.

To accept this as a statement of the essential thematic content of the novel is to concede that the novel is preachy: its didactic content lies on the surface to be skimmed off; one is not engaged in that act of imaginative response and re-creation that constitutes the entertainment value of a work of art. And what one skims off is a religious-ethical principle expressed explicitly in the novel, particularly by F. Alexander—"A man who cannot choose ceases to be a man."[2]

But this isolable ethical premise can be taken as both the explicit and implicit thematic content of the novel *only* if one assumes, as Burgess's comments lead one to assume, that *A Clockwork Orange* is merely a didactic novel with conventional satiric aims, a piece of conventional-formula satire whose explicitly enunciated norm provides the standard by which the satirist condemns the denial of free choice. Other assumptions are possible, assumptions that evolve from within the novel when one responds to its techniques and form, resisting both Burgess's stated intentions and the apparent confirmation of those intentions in the surface content.

The final chapter heightens one's awareness that more is going on in the novel than Burgess's stated intentions embrace, primarily because in the final chapter the integral techniques of the novel and its organic form are fully realized—*and not until then*. Only with the final chapter can one respond to the *total* conception and execution. One is stimulated to engage in the re-creation, in all of its subtlety and complexity, of the total imaginative act that the novelist's commitment to technique has realized.

THE IMMANENCE OF EVIL

Consider the point of view. Beyond a doubt, it commands great attention, since Alex as first-person narrator controls the novel. Though anyone reading the truncated version can hardly fail to respond to the vividly pervasive presence of Alex as actor and narrator, particularly to the egocentrism manifested in his behavior and commentary as well as in the self-conscious artistry of his narrative style, the deletion of the last chapter deprives readers of clarification of the inner springs of his act of artistic creation. Why does he tell his story? What does the compulsion to tell it reveal about his character? What meaning inheres in his mode of narration? Without the last chapter, readers are likewise left without the evidence needed to confirm or refute the impression made by his egocentrism that he is not a reliable observer of or commentator on his own behavior or that of others. Deprived of any indication of Alex's state of mind at the time of creation, one is denied the possibility of reflecting on the implications of the first-person narration, denied, in other words, the true import and impact of the organic whole.

To read chapter seven of part three is to become aware of profoundly disturbing implications and on reflection ultimately to realize that the novel *is* its telling. The final chapter allows one to discover that, unconsciously, Alex's creative act is an act of evil, an expression of immanent evil more frightening and more powerfully affective than the whole series of violent acts that he has overtly committed. And there is potent irony in this indulgence in evil at the precise point in his life when he believes he is finally opting for the good, an irony that delivers an emotional and intellectual impact far more provocative and stimulating than the end of chapter six, never intended by Burgess to be the climax of the novel. The ending of chapter six is a piece of deliberately contrived melodrama, and it is *wrong* as the climax of the novel. Alex's reveling in becoming his evil self again—"I was cured all right"—as he once more slooshies Ludvig Van and viddies himself "carving the whole litso of the creeching world" (p. 179) may move the libertarian to ecstatic celebration of individual freedom of choice, but it is a false climax, conducing to an orgy of self-congratulation and allowing the neat packaging of superficial ethical principles. The true climax, in chapter seven, does what I think Burgess intended to do: precluding both self-congratulation and the simplistic formulation of isolable themes, it distresses the reader into disturbing reflections on the nature of man.

In the final chapter, Alex is eighteen years old, the oldest and the leader of his new droogs. Only in minor ways has Alex's life-style changed: the droogs peet moloko with knives in it and the old violent in-out, in-out and tolchocking and dratsing are the usual evening's entertainment. But Alex feels bored and hopeless; he is growing mean, selfish, and soft, and can not understand why. He listens to malenky romantic songs, carries a photograph of a baby clipped from a newspaper, and sees himself as an old man sitting by a fire in an armchair, drinking tea. A chance meeting with his former droog Pete helps him understand his malaise and inarticulated yearnings. Pete, nearly twenty, is married and works for a state insurance agency; on this evening he and his wife are going to a wine-cup and word-game party. Alex realizes that he is growing too old for the sort of life he has been leading, and visions of a wife and son to come home to fill the hollow he feels inside. He must join the natural cycle, put his youth behind, and start the new chapter of his life with a search for a mate. He now can answer the recurring question ("What's it going to be then, eh?"): "That's what it's going to be then, brothers, as I come to the like end of this tale." This, then, is his frame of mind as he writes his story, the attitude of one no longer young—"Alex like groweth up, oh yes"— re-creating his youthful past and looking forward to a fruitful stage in the cycle of life to which he gives himself:

> Tomorrow is all like sweet flowers and the turning vonny earth and the stars and the old Luna up there and your old droog Alex all on his oddy knocky seeking like a mate.[3]

There seems little doubt that Alex's desires to produce a son and to write his story are analagous manifestations of creativity. To see that natural reproduction is a good is not difficult; to see that artistic creation is an expression of Alex's evil self, one of many acts of evil that he will very likely commit as a responsible, domesticated adult and good citizen, requires of one only the imaginative response demanded by the style and content of the story he has written.

The style of Alex's narration at eighteen years of age is, of course, a style created by Anthony Burgess at forty-two or -three years of age. The implications of this fact I shall explore fully later, but it should be kept in mind as I examine Burgess's explicit statements about what he wanted that style to accomplish. The integral functioning of the style he created for Alex reveals a great deal about Alex *and* Burgess, *and* ultimately oneself.

Burgess says that the language he invented for Alex to speak has a triple function: to assure the survival of the novel by creating a slang idiom for Alex that would not grow stale or outmoded as real slang does; to brainwash the reader so that he emerges from the novel with a minimal knowledge of Russian; and—of the greatest significance, it seems to me—"to distance the violence, to cushion the reader from the violence because the violence would not be presented directly [but rather] through a filmy curtain of an alien language that the reader would have to fight through before he could get to the violence.'' In his remarks on the glossary appended by Stanley Edgar Hyman to the American (Norton) edition, he complains that the glossary defeats his purpose, emphasizing what he led me to believe was the transcendent artistic motivation for the creation of Alex's language: he wanted the reader to respond imaginatively, creatively to the language in context, to hear its sound rather than pay attention to its meaning.

Of course, the glossary should be torn out of the Norton edition, as Burgess asks readers to do. But when one understands the implications of his contention that the language ''distances'' the violence, one has to conclude that the *language itself must be torn out* of the novel if readers are to be *kept at* a distance from the violence. Actually, the language intensifies and deeply involves readers in the violence.

One of the implications becomes clear when the paradoxical meaning of Burgess's intention ''to cushion the reader from the violence'' is grasped. He appears to be saying that the reader is *protected from* the violence; and in a superficial and deliberately deceptive sense he speaks truthfully: to read of Dim's swinging his oozy beautiful in the glazzies is not to visualize Dim's chain striking his victim's eyes. The language does appear to keep one at a distance from the gruesome brutality of the action. But rather than protect one from the violence, the ''filmy curtain of an alien language'' in effect *leaves one defenseless against it*. Were one to read in standard English of Alex's slashing Billyboy's face with a razor, one would be protected from the violence, distanced from it by his horror at Alex's savagery, complacent in his moral superiority and self-congratulatory in the knowledge that he could never do anything so savage. But readers have no such ego defenses against violence if they read of Alex's making this like veck creech when he viddies a nozh razrezing his litso and sending curtains of krovvy down his plott. Readers are seduced by the alien language to participate in the violence, to delight in the savagery of the scene, without being aware that they are giving expression to their own savagery. Awareness comes upon reflection: to see faintly through that filmy curtain has been, one realizes, to look into a mirror in which one sees one's own worst self.

If one examines the implications of Burgess's stated desire to have readers hear the *sound* of Alex's language rather than pay attention to its meaning, one can understand how Burgess robs readers of their defenses and forces them to confront their true selves. Burgess consciously created for Alex a *poetic* language: from the Russian he invented *groodies*, he has said, because the word better suggests fullness and roundness than does the English *breasts*; and the word *plott* for *body* sounds like a body being hit. This onomatopoetic quality of Alex's language, precisely because it does seductively invite readers to respond to its sound, is the major reason for my assertion that rather than protecting one from the violence, the style Burgess created for Alex immerses one in it.

By creating for Alex a poetic language, Burgess has endowed Alex with all of the resources of a vividly affective mode of expression. He has created in Alex a poet of violence. It would be futile to paraphrase a passage and expect to reproduce the effect of Alex's expression. Instead, listen to Alex's style as he narrates the attack on F. Alexander:

> [Dim] went grinning and going er er and a a a for this veck's dithering rot, crack, crack, first left fistie then right, so that our dear old droog the red—red vino on tap and the same in all places, like it's put out by the same big firm—started to pour and spot the nice clean carpet and the bits of his book that I was still ripping away at, razrez razrez. (p. 22)

The visual and auditory images are powerful, not only the vivid onomatopoetic creation of the noises Dim makes and the rhythm of his blows striking Alexander, but the metonomy of *red* for *blood*; the concreteness of the diction (*fistie, pour, spot, carpet, ripping*) coupled with the alliteration of *bits of his book* and *ripping* and *razrez*; the connotative power of *veck* and *dear old droog the red*, conveying frightening yet, paradoxically, attractive attitudes (surely a *veck* is a thing, not a human being, and who is so dull as not to respond intensely to the image of the shedding of blood as a communion with an old friend?); and the metaphor of blood as wine flowing from barrels.

This poetic expression is Alex's typical style:

> So I yelped: 'Out out out out!' like a doggie . . . . (p. 4)

The stars stabbing away as it might be knives anxious to join in the dratsing. (p. 16)

He tried to drink in all the blood from his wrist and howl at the same time, and there was too much krovvy to drink and he went bubble bubble bubble, the red like fountaining out lovely . . . . (p. 54)

The effect of his style, immediately and cumulatively, is to make readers respond intensely to its poetry, ego defenses neutralized by the delight one takes in the language. One is not distanced from the violence, he is immersed in it. The reader can not escape to the comfort of being a mere observer.

And this emotionally stimulating poetic expression is only one of the forces that engage one in the violence of the novel, for Burgess has endowed Alex with more than just the style of a poet: he has consistently characterized Alex as a poet, an artist. The style *is* the man. It is to the creative artist and his vision of the world that one continuously responds. Alex is thrillingly alive, acting in and reacting to the human world with supercharged sensibilities. He is repulsed by the reduction of a human being to a thing, whether it be his own refusal to be treated as if he were a thing or his intense dislike of human beings who turn themselves into things, although his language, to one's pleasure, reduces his victims to senseless objects. Of the man on a drug trip in the milkbar, he says, " . . .he had that pale inhuman look, like he'd become a *thing* . . ." (p. 26, his italics). His disgust at drunks—"I could never stand to see a moodge all filthy and rolling and burping and drunk . . ." (p. 13)—is in part a reflection of this attitude; but it is equally as much the adverse reaction of a refined aesthetic sensitivity. He can not stand Dim's animality, dirty or slobbery people, or offensive smells. To be sure, Alex's love of Mozart and Beethoven is a thematic device of Burgess's designed to link the heaven of music with the hell of violence; but it *is* rooted in Alex's character: it is a convincing manifestation of Alex's aesthetic response to life. And that is not a mere passive response to beauty: his ability actively to create beauty is evident in his re-creation in words of the sound of music:

Oh, it was gorgeousness and gorgeosity made flesh. The trombones

crunched red gold . . . , the trumpets three-wise silverflamed . . . . And
then a bird of rarest spun heavenmetal, or like silvery wine flowing in a
spaceship, gravity all nonsense now, came the violin solo . . . . Then
flute and oboe bored, like worms of like platinum, into the thick thick
toffee gold and silver. (p. 33)

His own acts of violence are like works of art, planned with exquisite
care and attention to detail, executed with conscious style: "it was a real
satisfaction to me to waltz—left two three, right two three—and carve left
cheeky and right cheeky" (pp. 16-17). His disapproval of the greed of his
droogs who want to go after the big money suggests that the pleasure Alex
takes in beautifully executed acts of violence is a manifestation of art for
art's sake, heedless as he is of both financial recompense and the opinion
of the world. Self-expression and self-assertion are his fundamental
attitudes, sufficient unto themselves as long as he is able to impose upon
the flux and variety of human experience his own control and order. His
narration has the quality of a lyric poem that evokes profound emotional
responses to its imagery and impresses deeply upon the reader the
personality of the poet.

It is a consummate act of perverse creation that compels readers to
delight in the violence that man commits upon man and to respond
positively, even with elation, to the desecration of human values that man
presumably cherishes. It invites one to celebrate his own worst self.

The final chapter, then, exposes a profoundly disturbing juxtaposition,
the resonance and ramifications of which are vastly different from those
of the melodramatic false climax of the preceding chapter. The Alex who
believes he has put violence and evil behind him, who sentimentally and
romantically envisions himself at one with the flowers, earth, stars, and
moon, and who is in search of a woman with whom he can lead a
peaceful, fruitful life, unwittingly reveals his true, unalterably evil self.
Alex has grown up, all right, but he is oblivious to the evil that he will
never outgrow.

In this way, then, by carrying the reader through to the full realization
of the novel's dominant technique, does chapter seven of part three
clarify the inner springs of Alex's act of artistic creativity. And by
suggesting that Alex is oblivious to its evil source, the final chapter also
clarifies and confirms the impression made by the truncated version that

the "humble narrator," no matter how reliably accurate and concretely exact his story, is an unreliable commentator: incapable of comprehending his own evil nature, he is therefore capable only of offering platitudes and dimly perceived half-truths about the nature of evil. For in the final chapter Alex reveals an inability to grasp *the implications of the content* of his story as surely as he is unable to grasp the implications of his style of narration. The *content* I refer to includes the two major subjects of his story, his own acts of violence—the tolchocking, the dratsing, the old in-out, and every other manifestation of evil behavior—and the acts of violence committed by others, largely adults in positions of responsibility and authority, which as well must be characterized as manifestations of evil.

Alex's story contains numerous instances of the violence and evil of the adult world that he is subjected to. Surely Dr. Brodsky's calculated effort to deprive Alex of the capacity to choose evil constitutes, as Burgess remarks, the ultimate evil. Dr. Brodsky and the Minister of the Interior have not been hurt or even inconvenienced by Alex; the evil they subject Alex to is merely a means to their own selfish ends. Those who have directly felt the effects of Alex's violent behavior, F. Alexander in particular, and another of his victims, the "starry prof-type" whom Alex attacked on his way home from the library, have, as it is said, "good reason" to seek retribution against him. But, of course, that "good reason" is a thirst for blood vengeance as barbaric in its essence and as savage as any act that Alex himself has committed. And one can not overlook F. Alexander's friends da Silva, Rubenstein, and Dolin, who, without the "excuse" of personal vengeance, collaborate in and execute F. Alexander's urge to kill the one who has done him injury. Nor can one forget the eagerness with which the library companions of the "starry prof-type" join in the beating of Alex, an eagerness that suggests delight in violence more than it does selfless assistance to a friend in redressing his grievance against Alex. If one adds the prison guards, all the police, and P. R. Deltoid, there is in the *content* of Alex's story an extensive range and variety of violence, both individual and institutional, that establishes it as *typical adult behavior*. The content conveys the theme that adult man is a creature of violence.

And that is what the eighteen-year-old Alex of the final chapter fails to understand. Alex sincerely attributes his own evil to his youth—"And all it was was that I was young" (p. 196)—and expects only good in the future, in his adult life. He stresses the sincerity of that conviction by "realistically" recognizing that his son and his son's son will behave in their youth just as he did in his. The truth established by the content of his own story and reinforced by its style and by the very fact that he writes it all is that the inherent evil of man will manifest itself no matter who he is or how old he is.

The author of the novel, in his early forties at the time of writing, realized this truth. He *did* participate in evil as the writer ultimately responsible for the celebration of evil created by Alex. Or, to be more accurate, he knew that he had to participate in evil, to give expression to his Alex-self, to revel imaginatively in savagery, in order to compel readers to revel in it. Since his ultimate purpose was to compel readers to delight in violence and thus to seduce them into giving expression to their own worst selves, so that they would have to confront the worst in themselves, their capacity for savagery, Burgess had to delight in savagery himself. He could not allow any hint of his own detestation of violence to creep into the narrative to alert ego defenses against violence. And that meant that he had to suppress deliberately his own ego defenses, to overcome his abhorrence of savagery. He has said:

> I had to get solidly drunk before I could sit down to a long description of rape, or of mayhem, or of murder.

Getting drunk was his means of overcoming the loathesomeness of violence, of releasing, for conscious artistic purposes, his own capability to commit, imaginatively, the violence that Alex commits and for enjoying the expression of his savage self.

The novel provides ample internal evidence that Burgess was fully aware of the necessity for and the implications of his participation in evil. I refer to the striking pertinence of the aesthetic-ethical issues that he has incorporated in part two, in those scenes dealing with the role of the artist in an artistic medium analogous to fiction—the film—and analogous to the content of Burgess's own novel—the films of violence used by Dr. Brodsky in his application of Ludovico's Technique. Alex explicitly raises some of the issues himself. In the first session of film showing, Alex thinks about the making of a film depicting a gang rape:

> This was real, very real, though if you thought about it properly you couldn't imagine lewdies actually agreeing to having all this done to them in a film, and if these films were made by the Good or the State you couldn't imagine them being allowed to take these films without like interfering with what was going on. So it must have been very clever what they call cutting or editing or some such veshch. For it was very real. (p. 103)

Alex has raised some penetrating questions but has failed to think of the major one: real or not, was not the violence in the film *created* by the "Good or the State"? And one can further ask: has not Burgess given a glimpse of his own agonizing awareness that he is the source of the real violence committed by Alex in the novel?

A related issue is suggested by Alex's judgment on the persons responsible not only for making but also selecting and screening the films:

> I do not wish to describe . . . what other horrible veshches I was like forced to viddy that afternoon. The like minds of this Dr Brodsky and Dr Branom and the others in white coats . . . must have been more cally and filthy than any prestoopnick in the Staja itself. Because I did not think it was possible for any veck to even think of making films of what I was forced to viddy . . . . (p. 106)

Are not those who participate in the making and showing of violent films themselves violent men? Drs. Brodsky and Branom are, to be sure, self-deluded perpetrators of the violence they deplore. And just as surely, Burgess is fully aware that he has given expression to his own "cally and filthy" mind in having created the potently vivid, filmlike, realistic scenes of violence in *A Clockwork Orange*.

I can abstract farther-reaching ethical issues from Dr. Branom's explanation to Alex of the purpose of Ludovico's Technique:

> What is happening to you now is what should happen to any normal healthy human organism contemplating the actions of the forces of evil, the workings of the principle of destruction. You are being made sane, you are being made healthy.

When we're healthy we respond to the presence of the hateful with fear
and nausea. (p. 108)

Are readers to suppose that Drs. Brodsky and Branom are healthy and
sane according to their own conception of sanity, that they themselves
react to the films with fear and nausea; or are they scientifically objective
and therefore indifferent to the films; or do they *enjoy* viewing the
violence in the films? Has not Burgess invited readers to apply the same
questions to *his* attitude toward the violence he created in *A Clockwork
Orange*?

He has confessed to his capability for creating and enjoying savagery
as surely as the narrative indicts Drs. Brodsky and Branom and the
"Good or the State" of unwittingly creating and delighting in violence.
Of course, in these admissions of his capacity for violence, Burgess has
confirmed his health and sanity. He can see and face the truth of his
human nature. A "healthy human organism," just as Dr. Branom's
pseudobehavioralistic principle maintains, *does* "respond to the presence
of the hateful with fear and nausea": it was precisely this fear and nausea
that Burgess had to overcome by getting "solidly drunk" before he could
describe the "hateful" violence of the novel. Yet I have to speak of Dr.
Branom's conviction as a *pseudo*behavioralistic principle because only
ideally is it true: he and Dr. Brodsky do not respond to violence with fear
and nausea. They are as unhealthy as Alex, who feared a chemically
induced nausea, not the violence in the films.

Burgess knows that healthy human beings, that is, those who are aware
of their capacity for evil, *do* contemplate the "actions of the forces of
evil" and "the workings of the principle of destruction" every day of
their lives. They need only contemplate themselves, as Burgess has, to
understand that evil is immanent in the nature of man. To grasp this
profound implication is to penetrate to the deep thematic heart of *A
Clockwork Orange*, to its tragic vision of humanity. Burgess has attempt-
ed to confront readers with their own worst selves, to force them to
agonize over their inevitable failure to be what they ought to be—good
men—an inevitable failure because men all have a capacity for evil. That
attempt is the measure of Burgess's own agonizing awareness, and it is
testimony to his never-ending struggle to preserve that tragic vision, as

ego-shattering as it may be. Constantly tempted to deform reality by taking comforting refuge in fantasy, in the illusion that he is a good man incapable of evil, he has forced himself to confront his own worst self, to contemplate the "actions of the forces of evil" manifested in his creation of the evil of Alex. The novel that helps one retain a grasp on the reality of human nature is itself a deeply moving documentation of its author's struggle to maintain his grasp.

THE PREVALENCE OF ILLUSION

Such contemplation of one's true self, however, is rare. *A Clockwork Orange* conveys Burgess's conviction that few know and even fewer care to know and face the truth of their evil nature, that man constructs illusions to hide from this truth. The novel introduces illusion after illusion representative of universal conceptions of human nature and ideals of conduct, and the satirist Burgess strips away each one, typically by revealing in traditional satiric manner the discrepancy between the illusory conceptions and ideals and the real nature of man manifested in his actual behavior.

Nowhere is this satiric process better illustrated than in Burgess's relentless undercutting of F. Alexander. The ideas expressed in F. Alexander's book, also entitled *A Clockwork Orange*, and certain convictions he expresses in person suggest that he is a spokesman for Burgess's own beliefs. In an excerpt from F. Alexander's manuscript that Alex reads at the time of the brutal attack on the Alexanders, one reads in essence what Burgess has publicly proclaimed as his intention in writing the novel: F. Alexander opposes "The attempt to impose upon man, a creature of growth and capable of sweetness, . . . laws and conditions appropriate to a mechanical creation . . ." (pp. 21-22). Later when Alex reads the published book, he summarizes its content as "that all lewdies nowadays were being turned into machines and that they were really . . . more like a natural growth like a fruit" (p. 159). And in conversation with Alex, reacting to Alex's account of Ludovico's Technique and its effect, F. Alexander speaks of the conditioned Alex as "a little machine capable only of good" and adds in words almost identical to Burgess's, "But the essential intention [of the conditioning] is the real sin. A man who cannot choose ceases to be a man'' (p. 156). F. Alexander seems to embody the Lancashire Catholic self of Anthony Burgess.

But seen in their contexts, both the stylistic context of the ideas expressed in Alexander's book and the situational context of Alexander's actions, Alexander's beliefs are revealed as self-delusions, sharply in contrast to his actual behavior. When Alexander writes of his opposition to turning men into machines, the style of his expression reveals the excesses of a romantic fanatic: the sweetness of which man is capable is "to ooze juicily at the last round the bearded lips of God" (p. 21). That image, together with the pretentiousness of Alexander's conception of himself as a pen-wielding Don Quixote—"against this I raise my sword-pen"—evokes a reaction from Alex that has to be Burgess's and the reader's reaction, too: "Dim made the old-lip music at that and I had to smeck myself" (p. 22). And the reader's reaction must be the same as that of Alex when he summarizes what he later reads in Alexander's book, "that we all like grow on what he called the world tree in the world orchard . . ., and we were there because Bog or God had need of us to quench his thirsty love . . ." (p. 159). The reader does not need Alex to tell him that the book is "written in a very bezoomy like style"; Burgess expects readers not to "like the shoom of this at all" and readers, too, are to wonder "how bezoomy this F. Alexander really was" (p. 159).

If the style of Alexander's expression is not conclusive evidence that Burgess is exposing Alexander's self-delusions, the situational irony is unmistakable. At the very moment that F. Alexander denounces the conditioning that has deprived Alex of his freedom of choice and pronounces his conviction that "A man who cannot choose ceases to be a man," Alexander is denying Alex his freedom to choose. The scheme to drive Alex to suicide has not yet been devised, but Alexander does treat Alex as a thing—"I think you can be used, poor boy" (p. 156)—and he and his cohorts, holding Alex captive, force him to do as *they* choose. F. Alexander's use of Alex as a thing to be manipulated is evidently typical of his political tactics. In a frenzied, passionate statement of his convictions, F. Alexander exclaims,

The tradition of liberty means all. The common people will let it go, oh yes. That is why they must be prodded, prodded—

and Alex reports: "And here, brothers, he picked up a fork and stuck it two or three razzes into the wall, so that it got all bent" (p. 161). The ultimate irony is that the man who willfully, albeit unconsciously, denies freedom of choice to others is himself not free to choose. The animal imagery in the Minister's report to Alex that F. Alexander is "howling for your blood" is apt: possessed by his lust for blood vengeance against Alex, F. Alexander is a beast driven by his instincts, not a man at all according to his own formulation that "A man who cannot choose ceases to be a man."

In contrast to F. Alexander, the Prison Chaplain, who expresses the existential tenet in almost precisely the same words ("When a man cannot choose he ceases to be a man" [p. 83]), devoutly believes in it and is agonizingly aware that he can not choose what he thinks he ought—goodness. He is pathetic in his inability to realize his ideal; yet the pity one feels toward him, one comes to realize, is self-pity, for in his anguish one sees one's own human frailty reflected. Copious amounts of whiskey serve to dull but can not deaden his fear that his failure to serve God will send him to a Hell that he knows exists. He realizes that he is serving not God but the Warden (deified as "Himself") in order, as Alex puts it, to become "a very great chelloveck in the world of Prison Religion." And he knows that he has stooped to the despicable means of using Alex as an informer in order to get a "real horrorshow testimonial from the Governor" (p. 81), and that he has despicably evaded his moral responsibility to avoid imperiling his selfish career ambitions. He reveals this awareness when he says to Alex, " . . . do not, I pray, think evil of me in your heart, thinking me in any way involved in what is now about to happen to you," after having admitted that if he were to protest he would jeopardize his career (pp. 94-95).

The sincerity of the Chaplain's painful awareness of his pathetic inability to choose the good is shown in that scene where he does impulsively choose the good and becomes as much of a hero as Burgess portrays in the novel. His finest moment comes at the demonstration of the success of Dr. Brodsky's conditioning of Alex when he speaks out without regard for his career:

> He has no real choice, has he? Self-interest, fear of physical pain, drove him to that grotesque act of self-abasement. Its insincerity was clearly to be seen. He ceases to be a wrongdoer. He ceases also to be a creature capable of moral choice. (p. 126)

The Chaplain himself has ceased to be a wrongdoer; he has made a moral choice to speak the truth, possibly because in Alex's self-debasement he has seen a mirror image of his own past behavior and realized that his own "grotesque acts of self-abasement" were motivated by self-interest.

But the next and final scene in which the Chaplain appears, his visit to Alex at the hospital, implies that he is too weak to continue to live his finest hour. In this scene, Burgess subjects the Chaplain to compassionate satire, exposing the duplicity the Chaplain indulges in to ease the pain of facing up to his weakness. When the Chaplain says to Alex, "But I would not stay [at the prison], oh no. I could not in no wise subscribe to what those bratchnies are going to do to other poor prestoopnicks" (p. 171), Burgess clearly invites readers to suspect that the Chaplain *could not* stay at the prison. Evidently the Warden has fired the Chaplain, for Alex has told his readers that when the Warden heard the Chaplain speak out, he gave him "a look like meaning that he would not climb so high in like Prison Religion" (p. 127). The suspicion is confirmed by Alex's observation that the Chaplain is still drinking heavily (he gives off "a very like stale von of whiskey"). And his imitation of Alex's diction for the first time (the double negative, *bratchnies, prestoopnicks*) suggests that he is speaking Alex's language in order to make Alex think him sincere. The characterization of the Chaplain as too weak to live up to his convictions, drinking and lying to deaden his conscience, taken together with the depiction of F. Alexander's unconscious hypocrisy, gives Burgess's satire a range from the sympathetically mild satire on man's inability consistently to face the truth about himself, to incisively severe satirical exposure of the inevitable hypocrisy of man totally ignorant of the truth of his human nature.

And what is this truth, the conception of the nature of man that permeates the novel? Burgess has Alex and the Chaplain each introduce half of the truth, and depends upon the reader to form the whole truth. Alex believes, self-deceptively as shall be seen, that he has freely chosen evil because he likes it—"what I do I do because I like to do"—and attributes the origin of evil to God: "badness is of the self . . ., and that self is made by old Bog or God and is his great pride and radosty" (p. 40). The Chaplain, less confident than Alex, asks rather than pronounces, "What does God want? Does God want goodness or the choice of goodness?" (p. 95). He attributes the origin of goodness to God and in effect says of goodness what Alex has said of evil: "Goodness comes from within . . ." (p. 83), which is to say that goodness is of the self. Together their separate statements form the essential truth: good and evil are of the self. Man is both good and evil in and of himself.

Burgess's belief that psychically man inhabits a "dualverse" of good and evil is well known. But it is imperative to establish its organic functioning in *A Clockwork Orange* if one is to delve beneath the surface content and conventional satiric aims of the novel to realize the sophistication and complexity of Burgess's probing of the human condition, to grasp the full dimensions of his cosmic satire. The meaning inherent in the title itself is a good illustration.

The title has a dual significance, one an ironic commentary on the other. Clearly, and I think superficially, Burgess intends to imply the accepted meaning, as derived from the Cockney expression, "Queer as a clockwork orange," referring to the aberrant and the unnatural. This meaning embraces the conventional satiric aim of the novel, Burgess's judgment on the conditioning process Alex is subjected to, his condemnation of the imposition, in F. Alexander's words, of "laws and conditions appropriate to a mechanical creation" that render Alex a *clockwork* orange, a machine.

But to keep in mind Burgess's conception of man's dual nature is to grasp another, more profound significance, one that complements the conception of clockwork-orange man as a queer, unnatural product of conditioning and deepens the cosmic themes of the novel. Man is and always has been a clockwork *orange*, by nature. Man is the orange, the natural fruit, and one can infer that the epithet "clockwork" refers to the delicately balanced psychic mechanism of man's dual nature. Man's clockwork is the steady, rhythmic heartbeat of his psychic life, the tick and the tock of his good and evil urges. This internal mechanism operates without man's conscious awareness or control. His clockwork will malfunction if tampered with; it will stop if the tension of its psychic springs is relaxed.

The condition of Alex before and after being subjected to Ludovico's Technique well illustrates the implications of this alternate significance of the title. The Alex the reader sees at the beginning is a natural clockwork orange whose psychic mechanism is malfunctioning because it has been radically tampered with. Alex's inherent capacity for evil has been intensified into overt acts of destructive violence by the severity of the repressive conditions imposed upon him. The social conditions that Burgess depicts are but satirically heightened versions of those actual repressive conditions that exacerbate man's inherent capacity for evil by forcing it to break out in monstrously perverse ways. The state has regulated everyone's life; it has subjected the masses to dehumanizing flatblock living; it represses free speech and free expression of individuality; it deadens the mind. Moreover the state has enforced its repressive measures with a police brutality that borders on savagery. Oh, Alex is evil all right: the tolchocking and dratsing, the violent in-out, in-out, and the destruction of property are intolerable manifestations of an intensified natural propensity to evil that might have been contained had the state not acted blindly on the grossly mistaken assumption that man's capacity for evil can be repressed.

By tampering with Alex's natural clockwork, the state, considered collectively as the repressive forces of society, has rendered him incapable of normal behavior. The subjection of Alex to Ludovico's Technique is then ironically an attempt by the state to eliminate the monstrously unnatural evil that it is responsible for having created. The result of the conditioning process is the destruction of the clockwork altogether: almost literally, it renders Alex incapable of life. The elimination of his capacity for evil necessarily entails the elimination of his capacity for good. In its ignorance of the psychic symbiosis of good and evil, the state has murdered Alex.

With consummate satirical skill, Burgess has the murderer himself, Dr. Brodsky, the agent of the state, unwittingly convey to the reader the principle that explains why the elimination of evil constitutes the killing of the psychic life. In response to Alex's revelation that the conditioning has deprived him of the enjoyment of music, Dr. Brodsky states:

> Delimitation is always difficult. The world is one, life is one. The sweetest and most heavenly of activities partake in some measure of violence—the act of love, for instance; music for instance. (p. 115)

His statement is perfectly true, but Brodsky does not realize in the slightest how accurate an account he has given of the inextricable meshing of the good he wants to enforce and the evil he wants to eliminate.

The elimination of evil has effectively denied Alex any participation in the good and necessarily, therefore, of participation in life. It is impossible to conceive of a profession or avocation or pleasure that the conditioned Alex can engage in. Burgess provides two illustrations of this negation of life that upon reflection multiply to the thousands. Alex can not become a physician because upon simply leafing through a medical reference work he is made sick by the sight of wounds and diseases (the smell of old age and disease makes him sick, too); and he can not read the Bible because he is nauseated by references to "smiting seventy times seven and a lot of Jews cursing and tolchocking each other" (p. 142). He can not be a lawyer, social worker, teacher, or clergyman. All forms of art, not music alone, and all "the sweetest and most heavenly of activities," not just the act of love, are denied him. Himself incapable of violence, Alex can not even be a good samaritan to the bleeding victim of someone else's violence or even read about violence. He can not be good or even contemplate the good because he has been conditioned to hate the evil that is extricably enmeshed with the good.

The state has not simply transformed a human being into a clockwork orange, "a little machine capable only of good," as F. Alexander believes and as a superficial reading of the novel as conventional satire would lead one to believe. The state has destroyed the clockwork orange that is man. Alex speaks from the depths of a destroyed psyche when he says, "I want to snuff it . . . I've had it, that's what it is. Life's become too much for me" (p. 143).

Burgess sees no hope and allows the reader to see no hope that the Brodskys and the Alexanders of this world will ever comprehend their own behavior. They will continue to tamper with the clockwork of others and not only intensify and exacerbate man's naturally evil tendencies but also concomitantly obstruct the functioning of the good. They will never look inside and see themselves as clockwork oranges. The evil they do is a perfectly normal function of their natural human selves. Brodsky's delight in sadistically torturing Alex and in viewing the violence of the films he uses in that torture is at one with F. Alexander's lust for blood vengeance, and Alexander's violence is at one with the evil of the "learned veck," whose article Alex reads in the paper, who deplores the "shortage of real horrorshow teachers who would lambast bloody beggary out of . . . innocent poops and make them go boohoohoo for mercy" (p. 41). They are human beings, clockwork oranges all, destined to commit *ultimate* evils because they have no awareness of their own capacity for evil.

Recognition of this conception of man as a natural clockwork orange enables one to grasp the full, profoundly disturbing pessimism that gives the novel its terrifying power. And now one can understand why the final chapter of the novel is essential. It is the culmination of Burgess's exposure of the illusions men live by and the completion of the expression of his pessimistic awareness of the difficulty or the impossibility of man's coming to realize and accept the truth that good and evil emanate from within the self. Though Burgess apparently approves Alex's "decision" in the final chapter to become a good citizen, he is in reality employing the first-person narration to alert the reader to the satiric vision that informs the whole novel. Alex shares in the illusions that his own story strips away. Though he believes sincerely and correctly that badness is of the self, he supposes that he is free to choose *either* good or evil, as if he could be one *or* the other. At fifteen he thought that to do evil was a choice he had freely made—"I do what I do because I like to do it." At eighteen he is equally deluded in his belief that he has chosen to be good, assuming that he can put his evil self behind him forever.

All along Alex has addressed the reader as his brother. Yes, in part one is Alex's brother, for the reader has expressed his own true self by delighting in the evil that Alex has indulged, in the writing of his story. But since the satirist in Burgess has seen to it that Alex's story is instructive, one has been granted the awareness that can prevent one from continuing to be the brother of the deluded Alex. To read *A Clockwork Orange* is indeed to participate in the sweetest and most heavenly of activities, for one has partaken of evil and simultaneously experienced the good.

NOTES

1. Mr. Burgess joined my seminar on the contemporary novel and gave a public lecture at Bucknell University on 15 April 1973. Notes of his responses to my questions in the seminar and a recording of his lecture are the sources of all statements attributed to him.
2. For obvious reasons, I am forced to cite the Norton edition of *A Clockwork Orange* (New York: 1963), p. 156. Hereafter, the page number will be given in parentheses in the text.
3. (London: William Heinemann Ltd., 1962), p. 196. Further references to chapter 7 of part 3 will be given by citing the page number of the Heinemann edition in parentheses in the text.

3

GILES GOAT-BOY:
MAN'S PRECARIOUS PURCHASE
ON REALITY

A brilliant comic novel *Giles Goat-Boy* certainly is. Yet it is a great deal more than just a hilarious and witty romp through the vagaries of hero-hood and the insanity of modern life. Any reader of *Giles* who has followed Barth from *The Floating Opera* through *End of the Road* and into *The Sot-Weed Factor* senses, even if he can not articulate his perceptions, that in *Giles* Barth has taken a giant's step forward in the direction that the earlier novels have moved, toward a definition of man, his universe, and his plight. I believe that with this step he has arrived at that definition.

Giles is a true culmination in the sense that it coherently fuses a great many of Barth's ideas about the nature of man that gave the three earlier novels a philosophical substance and an emotional depth of great power. In *Giles* Barth has synthesized and, as it were, realized those ideas to produce a consistent and comprehensive insight into the condition of man in an absurdly meaningless universe. And for *Giles*, Barth has found or created the form needed for the organic development of this integrated vision of man's fate. Or it may be that the form served as the means of integration: the myth of the hero that Barth adopted as his framework may have revealed to him the possibility of so interrelating the conditions of men in all ages and cultures that the plight of modern man could be given

43

a profound and universally valid interpretation. The precise relation between the form and content of *Giles* is a difficult subject to essay, and the attempt is almost impossible without first establishing an interpretive base from which one can sally out to explore the vast reaches of Barth's architectonic imagination.

As a means of orientation, it may be best to begin with an account of the basic narrative structure of the novel. When reduced to its fundamental plot line, *Giles* is not much different from *The Sot-Weed Factor*; as J.B. of the "Cover-Letter to the Editors and Publisher" remarks, "One novel ago I'd hatched a plot as mattersome as any in the books, and drove a hundred characters through eight times that many pages of it . . . ." [1] This mattersome plot is, however, relatively simple in outline, like that of *Giles*. Each is a novel of initiation or education as conceived in the satiric tradition of Swift and Voltaire. By convention somewhat episodic, this plot sends the young and naive hero into a world where varied adventures and encounters constitute an educational process relieving him of his naivete and producing a maturity of sorts. For purposes dictated by his parody of the hero myth that serves as the structural matrix of *Giles*, Barth has created a naif who is not so much naive as ignorant of human affairs, a boy raised as a goat far from the world of men. And George the Ag Hill goat-boy is no passive pupil in the school of the world; as a self-styled hero, savior, and great teacher, he actively seeks and reaches an understanding of the world and man through experiencing the nearly catastrophic effects of his attempts to be a mover and shaper of human affairs.

This much may be clear to the casual reader, but *Giles* does not yield its true form and content to the casual reader. To understand the complex variations Barth has played upon this basic plot and to grasp their thematic implications, even the most assiduous and perceptive reader is hard put unless he has at his command a far-ranging knowledge of the mythology upon which the novel is built. For ease of exposition, the three basic mythological components of the novel will be explicated separately. Concurrent with this exegesis I shall attempt to isolate and describe the major structural principles of the novel and to draw inferences about its meaning and relevance. This process should reveal some of the subtle and complex interdependencies among its distinctive formal configuration, its satirical perspectives, and its commentary on the plight of man. The three components are: first, the Hero Myth, centering on Giles, Bray, and Anastasia as the major figures in Barth's thorough, intricately patterned parody of the myth of the hero; second, the Founder's Hill Myth, embracing Stoker and Lucius Rexford and exploring the myth of the devil; and third, the Boundary Dispute Myth, involving the rivalry between East and West and Barth's mythopoeic interpretation of that conflict.[2]

THE HERO MYTH:
ACCEPTANCE OF ONE'S HUMANITY—
"THAT'S HERO-WORK ENOUGH"

Barth's parody of the hero myth is both the basic structural principle of the novel and its matrix of meaning. Although the parody becomes quite explicit at times, particularly when Max Spielman and Giles discuss herohood, innumerable details and several of its large symbolic elements are left to the discovery of the reader. To trace the parody in detail or even to outline it briefly is a task for WESCAC. I must be content here to suggest how extensively Barth has manipulated the myth.

As embodied in the mythology of nations and tribes around the world, the story of the hero begins with virgin birth. The mother of the hero is a royal virgin, his father a king or god, and the circumstances of his conception unusual. At his birth, his father or maternal grandfather attempts to kill him, often because of a prophecy of the hero's eventual displacement of the father. Abandoned in the wilds or set afloat in a basket or box to die, the infant hero often has his leg injured in some way before he is discovered, spirited away, and raised by foster parents in a far country. Consider the birth of Giles. His mother is in name and fact a virgin, Virginia Hector, the unwed daughter of the Chancellor of New Tammany College at the time, Reginald Hector. "Seduced" by the lustful automatic computer WESCAC, she is impregnated by osmosis, as it were, without so much as a kiss. The maternal grandfather is fearful of Giles's Prenatal-Aptitude-Test phrase, "Pass All Fail All," and abandons him to die in WESCAC's tape lift, where, in that box- and basket-like cage, his leg is "bunged up" by the tape cans, resulting in a permanent gimp. A Negro assistant librarian discovers the infant hero there, rescues him, and carries him to Max Spielman at the goat barns, where he is raised as a goat.

As here grossly outlined, almost devoid of comic detail and presented in a strict chronological order that Barth restructures into intricate and suspenseful plotting, the birth of the hero is the first of the three rites of passage—birth, initiation, and death—that together form the whole myth. The second stage, that of initiation, begins with the hero's coming to manhood, when he receives the call to adventure and returns to the scene of his birth to fulfill his destiny; continues through a period of trial (tests, tasks, battles) and his victory over his enemies; and culminates in his marriage to the princess (the Queen Goddess of the World) and atonement with his father. Death, the third rite of passage, soon ensues. The hero loses favor with the gods or his subjects, is driven from the city, and on the top of a hill meets a mysterious death, usually by burning or being struck by lightning.

Barth has exploited the full spiritual implications of the hero myth: he has conceived of Giles as a cultural hero whose quest has profound significance for the welfare of humanity. The major spiritual dimensions of the myth can be briefly sketched. At a moment of spiritual and social crisis a hero arises whose destiny it is to bring about a rejuvenation. His quest—to seek the boon that will restore the world—is at once a search for the father-creator, for self-identity, and for the truth. In his way stands his greatest enemy, the dragon, who represents the old generation. As keeper of the past with a vested interest in maintaining the status quo, the dragon is a tyrant holding man in bondage and preventing rejuvenation. Having slain the dragon, the hero is qualified to face the supreme ordeal: the meeting with the Queen Goddess, world creatrix, *magna mater*, the source of life. In his marriage to the Queen Goddess, the hero replaces the Father; and in the love experience itself, he has an illumination of the truth and is reborn. Having supplanted the Father, he realizes that he and the Father are one: the Father and the truth he had sought were within himself all along.

Barth's hero, Billy Bocksfuss ("goat-foot," like Oedipus), takes the human name of *George* once he becomes aware of his humanity and later assumes the more meaningful name *Giles* (probably derived from Saint

Giles, patron saint of cripples and beggars, an Athenian of the seventh century then called *Aegidius*, "wearer of the aegis [goatskin]," an apt name for Barth's goatskin-clad, crippled hero), but the name has a deeper significance in the meaning of the acronym GILES: "Grand-Tutorial Ideal: Laboratory Eugenical Specimen." Since the semen constituting the GILES was "taken from all New Tammany males between puberty and senility" (p. 321/*361*), Giles's true father is not WESCAC, merely the instrument of impregnation, but collective man, with whose seed WESCAC infused Virginia Hector. Almost literally, then, *Giles* means *son of man*.

And in an almost literal sense, the quest of this naive, would-be hero is to discover what it means to be the son of man. Under the mistaken impression that WESCAC is his father and that the current international tension between East and West is the crisis he is destined to resolve, Giles rushes in headlong and Quixote-like nearly causes disaster before he comes to understand his true mission. The naif undergoes a process of maturation and self-realization culminating in his grasp on the realities of life and in a revelation that the true crisis is a spiritual one inherent in the nature of man. This process of self-realization entails his overcoming Bray, who represents the dragon forces holding man back from full awareness of life and from acceptance of human nature and man's fate, and his symbolic marriage to Anastasia, who represents the Earth Goddess in union with whom Giles experiences the creative force of human love, that brings him to full understanding of the nature of man.

The hero myth calls for a protective figure who provides the hero with amulets against the dragon forces and acts as mentor and guide. This is the role of Maximilian Spielman (whose surname probably links him to the *spielman* of ritual drama whose role is to lead the hero into the action eventuating in his death). Max's sounding of the blasts upon the shophar or ramshorn he fashioned from the horn of Freddie is the hero's call to adventure, which in the higher mythology is a call to respond to a spiritual crisis. In the Rosh ha-Shanah service, the three blasts of the ramshorn— *Teruah, Tekiah, Shebarim*—call upon Israel to rally to its God and exhort it to a spirit of self-analysis. These calls and their symbolic significance go unheeded, however, and Giles responds instead to the sounding of the EAT whistle—to a political crisis, which Giles must learn the hard way is merely a symptom of a spiritual crisis soluble only when man heeds the true call of the shophar to rigorous self-analysis.

In addition to his parodic role as the hero's mentor, Max has two other roles, both in what may be called the *allegory of modern life*, the tenor of all of Barth's mythological vehicle. Max represents the humanitarian-scientific community of the atomic age and the psychoanalytic community of Freudian psychiatry. He is portrayed as a German-Jewish scientist whose hatred for Nazi genocides is complicated by his self-hatred for having been instrumental in the nuclear annihilation of the Japanese. Discharged and banished on the grounds of questionable loyalty during the administration of Reginald Hector (Eisenhower, the McCarthy era), Max retires to the goat barns where his misanthropy flourishes.

In banishment, Max makes great advances in proctology, the satirical equivalent of Freudian psychoanalysis with its emphasis on anal-eroticism. His Maxim, "Der goats is humaner than der men, and der men is goatisher than der goats" (p. 7/*44*), may not be a direct parody of Freudianism; but along with another of his Maxims, "*Self-knowledge is always bad news*" (p. 84/*121*), it pretty well indicates the depths of misanthropy to which "plumbing the bottom of man's nature" may lead. With its echoes of the Oedipus tragedy, the latter maxim sums up a prevailing attitude that modern man shares with ancient man, an attitude that Max and his scientific and Freudian counterparts must somehow temper if they are to gain a balanced, sane perspective on the nature of man and thus to face life on realistic terms. The way in which Max's misanthropy is gradually transformed into a love of mankind without the loss of his awareness of man's goatishness, a transformation implying Barth's comment on all misanthropes, among men, is too complex to detail here. Suffice it to assert that his experiences lead him to heed the call of the shophar to self-analysis and self-awareness, and that he comes to love mankind the more he understands his own nature. His death by crucifixion (shafting) is a martyrdom he gladly welcomes as an expression of his love for mankind and an affirmation of his love of life.

Significantly, Max's martyrdom and Giles's final rout of Harold Bray occur almost simultaneously. Clearly, since Max has achieved self-realization and dies in confirmation of his newly gained awareness of himself and of the nature of humanity, the rout of Bray signifies Giles's final achievement of his own self-realization. The last obstacle to the fulfillment of the hero's quest has been overcome.

While Bray's parodic role in the hero myth as the dragon figure, the archenemy of the hero, is not in doubt, just what he represents allegorically and thus exactly what obstacle Giles has overcome is a difficult question. Since Barth seems to operate from the existential premise that God is dead, it stands to reason that the archenemy of a modern hero striving for identity and self-awareness would be organized religion and the established church, the agents propagating the illusory transcendentalism that exploits man's propensity to seek his identity and essence outside of the self. This interpretation of the role of Bray seems reasonable both in the light of internal evidence and in view of the meaning that the name *Bray* is likely to have for Barth.

The surname of this enigmatic figure is very probably that of Thomas Bray, an Anglican clergyman credited with the establishment of the Church of England in Maryland. Thomas Bray's extensive missionary activity in that colony, coinciding precisely with the historical setting of *The Sot-Weed Factor*, must certainly have become known to Barth during his research into Maryland's colonial history. For Barth to have associated Bray's name with the personification of the church in the present allegory is understandable: Bray is the founder of the Society for Promoting Christian Knowledge and the Society for the Propagation of the Gospel. Another society, the Associates of Dr. Bray, was formed to assist him in administering a legacy devoted to pursuing the conversion of Negroes and Indians. That the name appears as *Harold* instead of *Thomas* Bray may be accounted for by Barth's desire to avoid literal duplication and by the aptness of the name *Harold* itself: meaning literally "hereweald," "army power" or "powerful general," it well suggests the power and militâncy of the church.

That this is Bray's allegorical role is also suggested by some details of Barth's parody of the New Testament. Bray is patently portrayed as John the Baptist (a proph-prof, like "John the Bursar," pp. 510-11/*563*) and as the Antichrist ("antigiles"): Giles, the new Christ, calls him "my adversary" (p. 703/*759*). Like Paul's conception of Christ's adversary, Bray is that satanically inspired human being who, claiming divine worship, establishes himself in the temple and pretends to divinity. As Paul envisions Christ's annihilation of the Antichrist, so Giles routs Bray.

These two parodic roles coalesce and have their relevance in Bray's allegorical function as a personification of institutionalized religion, particularly the dominant religion of the West, Christianity. In every speech and action, Bray can be seen as an embodiment of ecclesiastical authority. Having announced at his first appearance, "I'll show all of you who believe me the way to Commencement Gate! I'm the way myself, believe me!" (p. 314/*354*), Bray proceeds to certify everyone, nearly every time quoting an appropriate passage of the Founder's Scroll (Bible). In effect, he deludes all by indiscriminately promising passage (salvation) to all. Having declared, "Tragedy's *out*; mystery's *in*!", Bray satisfies the people's desire for mystery and for miracles as signs of a supernatural agency beyond their world. Having announced, "I'm your Grand Tutor!", Bray establishes himself as an authoritarian figure and father image to whom the people rush to commit themselves, desperately flocking to him seeking promise of Commencement (rebirth into everlasting life). Like the church, Bray upholds the conventional morality on which continuance of the accepted social structure and way of life depends: in conjunction with WESCAC, which embodies the principle of Differentiation, Bray approves when Giles advises the absolute separation of good and evil (the Christian duality of God and Satan), and damns Giles when he advocates rejection of all distinction between good and evil. And like the church, Bray forms an alliance with the government and is granted recognition, powers, and privileges on the tacit assumption that he will in no way disturb or contravene established domestic or international policies; and to him, like the church, is committed the supervision not only of religious services but of the educational system as well. Bray's power over New Tammany College is an apt representation of ecclesiastical power.[3]

Since the allegory fuses the mythological dragon and the biblical Antichrist into the one role of the established church as the enemy of Giles, Giles's rout of Bray is in a sense the fulfillment of Voltaire's imperative, "Ecrasez l'infame!" The infamy of the church is its opposition to the fully realized life; it is an obstacle to man's understanding of himself and acceptance of his fate. Encouraging man's preoccupation with death and fostering his futile, desperate search for transcendental reasons for his existence, the church creates illusions that blind man to his true existence. It inhibits man's self-realization when it supports the illusion of a moral duality, portraying good and evil as universal, opposed principles or forces, whereas man must perceive good and evil as polarities of his own psyche, as inseparable elements of his own nature. It falsifies the terms of man's existence on earth by promising an eternity of life hereafter and deludes man by gratifying his desperate longing for an extraterrestrial paradise that is no part of man's fate. If life is to be understood and lived on its own terms, not on imagined terms, the illusory tenets of the church must be rejected; one must defeat the tendency in oneself to transfer to suprahuman authority the responsibility for the guidance and direction of one's own life. Giles personally manages to defeat Bray, but Giles knows that, years after the rout, the people still believe in Bray and await his reappearance: the Bray in man dies hard, probably never will die. If Bray did not exist, most people would have to invent him, for few will ever face the truth about themselves.

The import of Giles's rout of Bray seems clear: he has overthrown the illusions fostered by the church; he has faced the truth about himself. In the allegory of contemporary life, Giles is modern man, for whom heroism is a complete acceptance of his humanity and acquiescence in man's fate. Portrayed in Giles as he describes himself in the "Posttape" is a sobered and subdued man who has cast off illusion and rejected the vain pretense of the reformer and the vain ambition of the idealist, who has learned to accept both in himself and in others "the ineluctable shortcomings of mortal studenthood" (p. 700/*756*), and who is sustained not by dreams but by the possession of self-knowledge. Since *"Self-knowledge is always bad news*," since man can be defined as a potential for both good and evil, learning to accept oneself may not be pleasant; but the truth can give satisfaction and serve as a guide for the sensible conduct of one's life. To accept oneself, one must, as Giles overcame Bray, reject the established church because it exploits man's propensity to hide from the bad news, to escape reality.

Essentially, Giles's learning to accept himself is a process of humanization. Conceived in mythological terms, it is a process of rebirth, and in this process Anastasia figures prominently. The name *Anastasia* is Greek for *resurrection*, an apt characterization of her function in the parody of the hero myth as the Earth Goddess in union with whom the hero is reborn. In the hero myth, the Earth Goddess is the world creatrix, *magna mater*, source of life; and the hero's meeting with the Goddess is a test of his ability to win the boon of love, *amor fati* or love of life itself. Their sacred marriage represents the hero's total mastery of life: it is a union of opposites signifying the attainment of wholeness and completion, and constituting regeneration and rebirth.

In the belly of WESCAC Anastasia fulfills her functions actively and consummately (pp. 672-73/730-31); earlier she serves as the passive agent of Giles's partial illumination and "delivery" (p. 651/709). Called by Leonid "a Commencèd martyr" and by Peter Greene "a flunkèd floozy" because she has given of herself so freely, Anastasia is both, Giles suddenly realizes. He understands in a flash of illumination that like all the other fundamental contradictions of passage and failure, the contradictory judgments of Anastasia's character are equally true. He is released, "delivered" from the mind-forged manacles, one of which is the conventional morality that constrains man to view woman in the exercise of her sexual function as either blessed or damned. His delivery is an abandonment of the search for *the* Answer and an embracement of life in all its contradictory, inexplicable variety.

This flash of illumination, this "delivery," is in itself a partial rebirth, an intellectual enlightenment that goes a long way toward making Giles a new man by freeing him from the trammels of old modes of thought. It will be worthwhile to pause here to trace the stages of Giles's intellectual development toward this enlightenment, even at the risk of displacing Anastasia momentarily; for the significance of Giles's total rebirth in the arms of Anastasia will be lost if one does not fully grasp the import of this partial rebirth. Through Giles, Barth is commenting upon the potential rebirth of modern man, and in Giles's intellectual development Barth traces the progress of mankind toward an enlightened outlook on life. In this commentary Barth's satirical assessment penetrates deep into the reasons for man's benighted condition.

Giles's progress toward the truth is best seen by analyzing the changes in his tutoring. The three distinct phases of Giles's tutoring correspond to stages in the moral history of Western man: the past, the present, and a future that Giles sees little hope of coming to pass. The first is the period when Giles advises according to the principle of Differentiation (Passage is Passage, Failure is Failure), a period representing the moral absolutism of the past fostered predominantly by the Christian church, whose conception of the duality of good and evil embodied in God and Satan is equivalent to Giles's insistence upon absolute separation of the passèd and flunkèd. The second period represents the present, the age of moral anarchy and rejection of absolutes. During this period Giles advises all to ''acknowledge, embrace, and assert'' their natural inclinations and to abjure all discipline and distinction: passage and failure are the same, he argues, indistinguishable and equally unreal.

Both of these positions are stages in Giles's progress toward the truth. Each emanates from Giles himself in response to the problems of human conduct. The error that Giles makes as his tutoring proceeds is to assure himself that each position arrived at is *the only* Answer or the whole truth: he recapitulates Western man's error of assuming that the then-current value system and ethical code are the only truth.

The third and final stage is near at hand when Giles conceives of the separate validity of the two preceding answers or truths: ''Passage *was* Failure, and Failure Passage; yet Passage was Passage, Failure, Failure! Equally true, none was the Answer . . . '' (p. 650/*708-709*). The final Answer that comes to him at the moment of ''delivery'' is not only that they are different, nor only that they are the same, but also that both their sameness and difference are simultaneously true. Passage and Failure, good and evil, are different, just as, to use theological terms, God and Satan are different, yet they are the same: Satan is an accessory to God and an embodiment of the Tigerness of God, who is Tiger-Lamb. They are not strict opposites but polarities, together forming a unity in the harmony of opposites. Giles realizes that man is a microcosmic unity of Tiger-Lamb, of evil and good.

This discovery of unity in polarity Barth renders symbolically by incorporating ancient mythology in the design of the PAT device that Giles finally understands at the moment of delivery. One can grasp the structure and meaning of this device if one removes the Prenatal-

Aptitude-Test phrase, "Pass All Fail All," to reveal the

quadrated circle , ancient symbol of cosmic unity. The circle
alone, sometimes called the *Supreme Ultimate*, is that which contains all,
symbolizing wholeness or completeness. The halving of the circle represents the division of the primal chaos into apparently opposite forces that
are polarities harmoniously interacting to form a unity.

The multiplication of polarities in a complex system is symbolized in
the quadrated circle, which also represents the universe, with its center
(the *axis mundi* or world navel) marked by the intersection of lines drawn
from the four cardinal directions.

In the first stage Giles conceived of Passage and Failure as opposites,

different and separable, like white and black. In the second
stage, by rejecting all distinction and asserting that Passage and Failure
are the same, he set the circle in motion, as it were, making it spin so
rapidly that white and black fuse to grey, which, neither white nor black,
is a blurring of their real distinction. Finally he grasps the significance of
the PAT device, "beginningless, endless, infinite equivalence" (p.
650/*708*). His "delivery" is a recognition of the white, of the black, and
of the white-black, which though they "spin" never merge into grey.
Passage and Failure are two poles of a unity.

Though one can diagram this truth in oversimplified form, one does not
easily assimilate it into his being. As Giles realizes, it is a truth that can
not be taught; it can be grasped and assimilated only by a sort of mystical
insight and only by the individual who plunges into life with all of his
faculties alert and says, like Giles, "I must wrest my answers like Swede
roots by main strength from their holes" (p. 409/*455*).

Barth offers little hope that many people will try to or can earn the feel
of this truth upon their pulses, but Giles does make it a part of his being.

Its effect upon him is to bring instantaneous illumination, freedom, intellectual rebirth. But fully to comprehend the truth of his own nature and thus to find his identity as a human being—to be totally reborn— Giles must come to understand and integrate the emotional component of man. It is the function of Anastasia to bring about this ultimate comprehension, to complete the process of humanization. For Giles, Anastasia's repeated profession of love is the final mystery; "that final shadow" (p. 671/730) is his inability to understand the human need to love and to be loved. Her mysterious but unquestionably sincere professions of love lure Giles, draw him out of the shadow until the light of love finally wipes out the shadow. At last he understands what it means to be human.

The consecrative act confirming this understanding, the union of Giles and Anastasia in creative love, takes place in the belly of WESCAC, the very spot where Giles was conceived. To enter the belly, Giles and Anastasia ride down in the tapelift, symbolically for Giles a return to infancy and an approach to rebirth since he had been abandoned in the tapelift as a newly born infant. There is further symbolism in the position they assume in the tapelift: in its narrow confines, crowded "Knees to chin and arsy-turvy," they resemble not only twins in the womb but also "that East-Campus sign of which her navel had reminded" Giles earlier

(p. 671/729). That sign is the Tao, the symbol of cosmic order

sometimes called the *yin-yang* because of the union it represents of the masculine principle *yang* and the feminine *yin*. Incidentally, they are also in position 69, and the ribald comic tone of this tapelift scene is soon intensified when Giles and Anastasia form what may be the most hilarious copulation in literature: twined round Giles and impaled upon his member, Anastasia wears the mask of Bray; and Giles wears over his head a bag drawstringed around his neck. Masked and bagged, they tumble together through the port and slide down into the belly.

In the belly, scene of two premature abortive attempts at rebirth, Giles is reborn when he grasps the meaning of the unity that he and Anastasia have demonstrated coupled together in love: like *yin-yang*, they are male and female made one in the act of love, and Giles understands the macrocosmic implication of their microcosmic union—the universe is one. He experiences that expansion of consciousness that allows him to embrace all of the contradictions, the antagonisms and oppositions, the differences of all men and all nations as manifestations of a single life force. He embraces life.

The scene concludes with Giles and Anastasia in orgasmic rapture, he fully illumined, fully realized as a human being, fully in grasp of the mystery of life. He imbibes his divinity, which is humanity, from the "nipple inexhaustible" of the goddess; he then feeds himself; and together they cry, "Oh, wonderful!" (p. 673/*731*), chanting as one a "mystical rapture of the knower of universal unity" from the *Taittirìya Upanishad* (3.10.5-6):

> Oh, wonderful! Oh, wonderful! Oh, wonderful!
> I am food! I am food! I am food!
>
> I am the first-born of the world-order,
> Earlier than the gods, in the navel of immortality!
>
> I, who am food, eat the eater of food!
> I have overcome the whole world!

Anastasia, experiencing an orgasm for the first time in innumerable loveless copulations, receives the seed of humanity and, in love, conceives a child.

Giles is assured that he is indeed the Grand Tutor, yet ironically he can no longer tutor. He can not teach because the illumination he experienced in the arms of Anastasia can not be conceptualized, can not be taught. But others mistakenly assume that Giles's Answer can be codified and transmitted. Gilesianism is made out to be teachable doctrine, and a new religion is created. Giles explicitly disowns Gilesianism, speaking of it as Anastasia's "term, for her invention" (p. 700/*756*). But she and Peter Greene style themselves disciples of the New Christ and devote their lives to the spreading of "Giles's word."

But even they, who knew Giles intimately, disagree about just what Gilesianism is. Already, strong signs of factionalism, schism, and eventual strife herald for *The Revised New Syllabus* a fate like that of the Bible. It may be that Gilesianism will become, like Christianity, a battleground of contention because its disciples are guilty of oversimplification, prejudiced interpretation, or self-aggrandizement. Greene's formulation of Gilesianism, for example, seems to be based on his own life history: he says of his own attempt at rejuvenation, "I'm going to start from scratch, what I mean *understandingwise*" (p. 652/*710*), words translatable into the doctrine, "Become as a kindergartner." Thus formulated, the doctrine is a fair approximation of the experience Giles has undergone and of the gist of his illumination. It does suggest regeneration and rebirth in the recovery of lost or hidden dimensions of one's nature. And it suggests further the return to innocence accomplished by regaining the fully integrated personality that existed before the self was fragmented in its many attachments to the external world. But how does one teach people to become as little children? Giles knows that, like Buddha's Enlightenment, his Answer or truth is not communicable: it must be experienced, and only a few will ever have the illumination granted to him. Greene and Anastasia attempt to teach the unteachable.

Like other great teachers who intuitively grasped the need to reenter the microcosm of the self—the Grand Tutors Buddha, Socrates, Christ—Giles can leave behind him as his doctrine only the embodiment of the truth, his life as recorded in *The Revised New Syllabus*. The essence of true Gilesianism must be distilled from the story of Giles, just as the exemplary lives of the Grand Tutors both reveal and conceal the essence of their teaching. *The Revised New Syllabus* will be a further contribution to the body of wisdom available as a guide for humanity. It will join "such root pedagogical documents as the Moishianic Code, the Founder's Scroll, the *Colloquiums* of Enos Enoch, the *Footnotes to Sakhyan* [that came] from individual students who had matured and Graduated over the semesters [and are] the best Answers that studentdom had devised . . ." (p. 255/*301*). But Giles knows well that few will profit from this wisdom: the world will go on as it has for centuries.

In the Founder's Hill Myth that examines and defines the "diabolical" in human nature, Barth embodies the cosmic insights that underlie the satirical perspective conveyed through Giles's awareness that nothing will change.

THE FOUNDER'S HILL MYTH:
THE PSYCHIC TENSION BETWEEN GOOD AND EVIL

The hill bearing the Founder's Shaft and containing Stoker's Powerhouse located over a raging subterranean volcano is the parodic counterpart of the world navel or Primeval Hill of ancient mythology. A metaphysical point set at the axial center of the world (*axis mundi*), the world navel was established in ancient ritual as the source of creative energy, and there mysteries were performed celebrating the generation of life and the creation of the cosmos. It was ritualistically conceived as the connecting link among the three planes of existence, the sky world or Heaven, the Earth, and the Underworld. In Sumerian culture, the Primeval Hill, the fountainhead of emerging life, was given symbolic form in the ziggurat, the Mountain of the Gods connecting Heaven (the male principle) with Earth (the female principle) and with the Waters of the Abyss, the water of life. In the Garden of God on the Mountain was the World Tree, the tree of life, at whose annual waning the ritual king administered the food and water of life. In the "Posttape," Giles envisions a place much like this garden as the scene of his "turning off": "on the highest rise of Founder's Hill," where stands one oak and runs a spring, his end will come in flashes of lightning (p. 708/*764*).

But the Underworld is of greater significance than the summit of the hill. In Stoker's Living Room, where Earth and the Underworld meet, Giles joins Stoker's Spring Carnival Party and participates in a rite of renewal similar to the mystery celebrated at the world navel. The cycle of death and birth is celebrated in the literal cremation of the dead G. Herrold and in the homeopathic act of procreation as Giles "services" Anastasia in drunken animal abandon. Both of these mockeries prefigure real acts of fulfillment that occur, significantly, nine months later: Max is then cremated on Founder's Shaft in the same flame that consumed G. Herrold, but his death is a sacrificial crucifixion on behalf of mankind, and thereby a consecration of love and life; and Giles and Anastasia then unite in an act of love that constitutes the rebirth of Giles.

Stoker's Powerhouse, the cap on the volcano as he describes it (p. 178/*220*), is on the same level as the Living Room and appropriately so; for Stoker's role in the Living Room as master of the revels in the orgiastic celebration of life is one manifestation of his larger role as director and controller of the elemental power of the volcano, the source of creative energy, the life force. Literally, Stoker's Powerhouse supplies the power that lights the Light House, operates WESCAC and EASCAC, and in general runs the University; on a deeper level of meaning, Stoker controls the elemental energy that feeds life to the world. He is the embodiment of the life force that animates all men: without his power, there is only stagnation and death.

So fearful have Christian moralists been of the life force that they have called it *evil*, personified it in the devil, and then reviled it as the enemy of the good. To make Stoker recognizable as a force commonly thought diabolical, Barth has provided a few unmistakable signs: his surname seems to derive from his role as the devil who stokes the fires of hell, and, of course, he wears a "sharp beard, like a black spade" and has hornlike ridges of black hair "from the front of either temple up to his hairline" (p. 151/*192*).

But Stoker is not the Satan of Christian mythology. He is more like the god of the underworld of Greek mythology, terrible but just and not the enemy of man. Pluto-like, Stoker was stricken with a desperate love or need for the Earth Goddess Anastasia, who like Persephone satisfies his need of alignment with the feminine creative force of nature. And as director of the Powerhouse, he serves a Pluto-like function as a god of the fertility of the earth, controlling the flow of the life force to the world of men.

In the parody of the Bible, Stoker as Dean o'Flunks is satanic only in that he functions like the Satan of the Book of Job: he serves good by testing and tempting the righteous. Only in the eyes of the conventional moralists is he seen as the archenemy of the good: with his native insight, Giles senses immediately that "there was something *right* in Stoker's attitude" (p. 211/*253*). Right indeed, for Stoker is a personification of evil as interpreted by the most profound mythologies, particularly the Oriental, which conceive of evil as a pole of the good: evil and good together form the divine. But since in Barth's world the only divinity is man, Stoker is an embodiment of the evil emanating from *human* nature: *man's* inherent urge to live unfettered and unhampered by reason, codes of conduct, or any authority. He is the flunkèd in all men, the urge for disorder, the spirit of rebelliousness against order and authority. Ranging from mere obstreperousness, through calculated opposition, to a potentially violent destructive impulse, all inclinations to evil as manifested in Stoker can be seen as an irrepressible life spirit chafing at any form of restriction or containment. But the unrestrained life force is disruptive and chaotic; restriction and containment are necessary if society is to flourish. For good reason Stoker's authority is limited to the Powerhouse and Main Detention.

On the literal level of the narrative, the person who enforces this restriction of Stoker's authority is the Chancellor of New Tammany College, Lucius Rexford. *Rexford* seems to be a combination of Latin roots for "strong king," befitting his character and his position. In the allegory Chancellor Rexford represents, in particular, former President Kennedy and, in general, the world leader at a time of international crisis. Rexford's description of "the typical Graduate" (p. 368/*411-12*) fits Rexford himself and John F. Kennedy point for point; and numerous details about Rexford, including his physical appearance (unmanageable forelock of bright, fair hair), demeanor (grace, wit, and gusto) and thought (for example, his stress on physical fitness and intellectual development), confirm that Kennedy is the model for the largely favorable portrayal of Rexford.

But the contemporary political allusion to Kennedy seems almost incidental except insofar as it helps to establish *Giles Goat-Boy* as a commentary on contemporary life. Rexford is an allegorical modern leader upon whom rests the awesome responsibility of power; but he is first a man who must come to a realization of his own potentialities before he can function effectively as a leader and carry out policies designed to help mankind realize its potentialities.

This theme is conveyed through Barth's utilization of the mythological notion of the rivalry of two brothers: Rexford's first name *Lucius*, meaning *light*, corresponds to the first name of Stoker (*Maurice, dark*) to suggest the mythological role of Rexford and Stoker as the brothers whose rivalry represents the opposition between light and darkness. In mythology this rivalry symbolizes an ultimate cosmic unity: the brothers, apparently opposites like day and night, are better described as polarities; and their interaction is a harmony and balance like the life cycle of day-night.

Rexford has to learn to accept Stoker as his brother or other half without affirming the kinship; he can neither fight against him nor yield to his power. When, under the influence of Giles's erroneous first tutoring, Rexford denies his kinship with Stoker and kills Stoker's spirit by enforcing puritanical laws, the college stagnates and dies. Conversely, when Giles's second tutoring, also erroneous, persuades Rexford to embrace Stoker, openly avow kinship, and live like him, chaos results: the unrestrained life urge or evil runs rampant, threatening destruction of the college. The proper balance is achieved when Rexford reestablishes the rivalry and recognizes the necessity of allowing Stoker to function without Rexford's openly affirming their relationship lest Stoker gain dangerous prominence. In effect, he becomes a whole man who has struck the proper balance between his own good and evil proclivities. This balance becomes Rexford's political philosophy as well. In his moderate idealism tempered by a thorough grasp of realities and by his cognizance of the power of the life force and of its inclination to excess in all, even himself, Rexford can operate effectively as a consummate politician and as a consummate human being. This striking of the proper balance in Rexford is, of course, a variant on the major theme of the hero myth—Giles's achievement of wholeness and completeness as a fully integrated human being. And this theme emerges as the idea underlying Barth's portrayal of nearly every other character in the novel.

One not so subtle manifestation of the theme appears in the pairing of Croaker and Eblis Eierkopf. They form a very apt complementation of under- and overdeveloped mentality, of animality and rationality. The two are portrayed as a pair in an imperfect partnership that makes up a crude approximation of a human being. Croaker is reasonless animality in which love is an instinctual drive to tup, tup, tup. Lustless, emotionless Eierkopf, the former Bonifacist eugenicist who experimented with human subjects in the concentration camps, is an embodiment of heartless rationality, of the inhumanity of the disengaged intelligence and dispassionate scientific curiosity. Both are incomplete human beings; each needs the other to subsist.

A much more subtle and thorough exploration of the theme of consummate humanity is to be found in Barth's portrayal of Dr. Kennard Sear. Like the portrayal of Giles himself, the development of Sear traces the progress of an individual from ignorance of self to self-awareness; and, as is typical of Barth's utilization of mythology, Sear's character and plight are defined through comparison to a prominent mythological figure, Gynander (Teiresias).

The surname *Sear* is a play on at least two words: the adjective *sere*, suggestive of Sear's physical appearance of desiccation and of his sexual and spiritual sterility; and the noun *seer*, prophet or soothsayer, referring to his self-drawn comparison to Gynander. Like Gynander (from the Greek for *woman and man*) Sear is a hermaphroditic figure, and so, too, is his wife Hedwig. Both are bisexual, and their behavior gives the impression that her lesbianism and his homosexuality have been deliberately pursued as perversions to relieve the boredom that normal heterosexuality has long brought them. Both are connoisseurs, effete and sophisticated, who are driven in pursuit of hedonism to taste every perversion known to carnal man. Worst of all, they have perverted the principle of marriage: each uses the other as a means to gratify his sensuality.

Sear thinks his knowledge of the world comparable to Gynander's; but, as Giles makes clear, Sear mistakes extensive experience for comprehensive understanding. Unlike Gynander, who understood the whole man and his plight, Sear is surfeited with experience and loathes himself as he loathes all men because he attributes to them only the depravity he finds in himself. Yet, with the help of Giles's tutoring, Sear does become like Gynander. Finally, in blindness, Sear sees his failings clearly and comprehends the whole truth of human nature. He has learned that to come to his wife in simple love to beget a child would not be the "consummate perversion" for a man of his tastes but the consummate humanization. Though it is Croaker who impregnates Hedwig, Sear has recognized his love for her and their need to be together; he gladly accepts Croaker's child as his own in token of what should have been. Realizing that "spiritedness" or impassioned attachment to another human being makes life meaningful and worthwhile, he, at the point of death, is reborn as a whole man.

THE BOUNDARY DISPUTE MYTH:
THE PERILOUS BALANCE MEN MUST MAINTAIN

In the Founder's Hill Myth the rivalry between Rexford and Stoker is a parodic version of the ancient mythological conflict between two poles of the psyche that are integral components of the whole man. Similarly, the international rivalry between East and West is given mythical delineation as a competition for ascendancy between two dimensions of the mind. Man has always externalized his interior life by projecting upon the external world or macrocosm his own emotional stresses or psychic conflicts, as he has in representing the contrary moral duality of his own nature as a cosmic opposition between forces of good and evil. And often this kind of projection of the psyche's opposing components takes mythic form in images of opposition between nations.

Barth's mythopoeic imagination has conceived of the East-West rivalry as a conflict between man's inherent proclivities to selfishness and selflessness; or, to put it another way, this natural competition within the psyche is projected on a large scale as a competition between nations committed in principle to selfishness (capitalistic America) and selflessness (communistic Russia). That these nations represent poles of the psyche is suggested by the fact that one Control Room, located in Founder's Hill, channels Stoker's power to both East and West and operates both EASCAC and WESCAC. As Stoker says, "Me they have to put up with, like it or not . . . . They've got to have power if they're going to be enemies" (p. 176/*217*). The natural psychic conflict animated by Stoker's life force is that between a concern for the personal self (greed for material acquisition and insistence upon the inviolability of the individual will) and a concern for the group self (submission to the will of the group, whose welfare takes precedence over the individual's). Selfishness is caricatured in "greedy and grasping" Ira Hector, and selflessness in Classmate X, who eradicated his self and replaced his "personal, fallible will with the Will of the Student Body, impersonal and infallible" (p. 547/*600*).

Within this pattern of gross caricatures, two other characters—the American Peter Greene and the Russian Leonid Alexandrov—function as vehicles of a far more penetrating and subtle analysis of American selfishness and Russian selflessness than the caricatures allow. In this portrayal of these two exuberant and optimistic naifs, Barth seems to be exploring the effect of human love upon the dehumanizing pressures exerted by their respective societies.

In the trio of figures who serve as vehicles of Barth's satire on capitalism and the American way of life—Reginald and Ira Hector are the others—Greene represents the active, aggressive class of business executives and industrialists as distinguished from the financiers and speculators. He is a doer; he embodies the spirit of rugged individualism. His life history (pp. 228-46/*271-92*), an encapsulated allegorical his-

J. B. : "THE PERPETUAL POSSESSION
OF BEING WELL DECEIVED"

Numerous structural and thematic interrelations, previously presented, bind together the three basic myths of the novel into a coherent interpretation of the condition of man, each myth in its particular way exploring the components of the psyche as manifested in human affairs; that Barth's central concern is to illuminate mythopoeically the plight of man divided against himself and man divided against man; and that through a wide range of mythology—ancient and modern, pagan and Christian, Oriental and Occidental—Barth interprets the plight of man as a universal condition, universal because it arises from a fragmentation of the psyche witnessed in the myths of all ages and countries. Readers can then see that in J. B., I believe, Barth sums up, as it were, portraying a character of the present moment, outside the world of the novel proper, who epitomizes the condition and the plight of a contemporary Everyman. And in so doing, Barth projects the past and present into the future, implying that what has been and is universal will continue to be so.

To what degree one is to assume that in J. B. John Barth has portrayed his realistic awareness that he shares that condition and plight, I can not say. Certainly Barth identifies himself with J. B. in saying, "like most of our authors these days I support myself by preaching what I practice" (Preface, p. 18/22), and it takes no great stretch of the imagination to expand this autobiographical note to hear the voice of Barth in J. B.'s lament:

> My every purchase on reality—as artist, teacher, lover, citizen, husband, friend—all were bizarre and wrong, a procession of hoaxes perhaps impressive for a time but ultimately ruinous. (Preface, p. 23/28)

At times everyone senses that their hold on reality is "bizarre and wrong" and like J. B. "yearn to shrug off the Dream and awake to an order of things—quite new and other!" (Preface, p. 24/29). And in that yearning do not all admit to "the ineluctable shortcomings of mortal studenthood"? Has not Barth admitted that J. B. is a reflection of his—and man's—own desperate search for an "order of things," no matter how illusory that order may be?

At any rate, in J. B. Barth has epitomized the precariousness of the human purchase on reality and those weaknesses in man that militate against a true perception of reality, against self-awareness, and thus against fulfillment as integrated human beings. His attitude is the reason why man can not, unlike the extraordinary hero Giles, assimilate the wisdom of the ages and profit from experience to come to know himself. His spirit, while superficially exuberant and optimistic, creates the continuous tragedy that history records; and it blinds him to the tragic implications of his own unrealized life.

As an "aspirant professor of Gilesianism," J. B. is linked, almost equated, with Peter Greene and Anastasia, those disciples of the New Christ who in their desperate search for the Answer, for the comforting assurance of doctrine, effectually create a new religion and thus perpetuate the powerful urge in man to locate in suprahuman authority the reason for and explanation of his existence. Without awareness of what he is doing, J. B., like Anastasia and Greene, is invoking another Bray and confirming Giles's belief that Bray in one form or another will never die. Ironically, Bray will be re-created in the form of Giles. In terms of the hero myth, J. B. is creating another dragon, who will maintain the status quo of self-blindness by encouraging man's inherent tendency to hide from the truth about himself, to refuse to accept his fate. In short, Barth represents in J. B. an abbreviated etiological myth accounting for the existence of religion and its institutionalization. Man is too weak to live without the comfort of religion.

J. B.'s attribution to Giles of "joy, hope, knowledge, and confident strength" is symptomatic of an attitude that almost guarantees that man will never harmonize the polarities of his psyche, never integrate the Evil One, never know himself as a whole embracing good and evil. J. B.'s elevation of Giles to godhood as an embodiment of the good, taken along with his inability to see, let alone accept, the tragic implications of Giles's Grand Tutorhood, is representative of the powerful human tendency to leap to any judgment that will put the most favorable interpretation on the nature of man. Anthropomorphically, J. B. has created a god in his own mistaken and shallow image of himself. The difference between the real Giles and J. B.'s creation is the measure of J. B.'s refusal to face the truth about himself. The inevitable consequence of this attitude will be the propagation of that consistent error that Barth made clear in his portrayal of Stoker: refusing to locate the source of evil either in Giles or himself, J. B. will re-create the devil as an embodiment of the evil he knows to exist; and the resulting moral duality will be the projection of his own failure to harmonize the poles of his own psyche. That this age-old psychic split is at work in J. B. is evidenced in the "Postscript" by his identification of the enemy, as yet undefined but powerful in potential, an "antigiles" to whom he attributes the concoction of the "Posttape" as an attempt "to gainsay and weaken faith in Giles's Way" (p. 710/766).

In J. B. Barth has created an all-too-typical human being who, finding the truth unbearable, refuses to see it and erects potent illusions that will comfortably serve as substitutes for the truth. J.B. is a persona created to speak for those whose happiness consists in the *"perpetual Possession of being well Deceived."* Barth's insight into the condition of man is very much like Jonathan Swift's, from whose *A Tale of a Tub* I have just quoted. *Giles Goat-Boy* offers at its core a satirical view Swiftian in its intensity and profundity, a moral realism that begs man to see himself as he truly is, a satirical view transformed to the tragic, as it is in the *Tale*, by the pervasive implication that man has so thoroughly accustomed himself to live by illusion that the satirist has little hope of ever seeing that illusion stripped away. This is the tragic burden of Barth's comic novel.

NOTES

1. *Giles Goat-Boy* (Garden City, New York: Doubleday and Company, 1966), p. 20/*24*. Further references to *Giles* will be made in the text by citing in parentheses the page number of the 1966 edition, followed in italics, as above, by the corresponding page number in the paperback edition (Greenwich, Connecticut: Fawcett Publications Inc., n.d.), since it may be more readily available.
2. Perhaps I have done just what Robert Scholes warned against in *The Fabulators* (New York: Oxford University Press, 1967), p. 170: "to take the mythography of *Giles Goat-Boy* in too heavy a way would do the story violence." Since my study was completed in essentially its present form in 1966, within a few months of the publication of *Giles*, the warning came too late. I remain convinced that the mythography must be taken "heavily." See Scholes's excellent chapter on *Giles*, pp. 135-173; I find his approach a valuable complementation to my own.
3. This church-state dimension of Bray's role calls to mind the anonymous eighteenth-century poem "The Vicar of Bray" as a possible source of the name Bray. Barth has Ebenezer Cooke use the Vicar of Bray as a metaphor in *The Sot-Weed Factor*. The speaker of the poem, the Vicar, recounts the opportunistic shifting of allegiances he indulged in to gain preferment from whatever monarch ascended the throne.

4

SLAUGHTERHOUSE-FIVE:
LIFE AGAINST DEATH-IN-LIFE

"He's the greatest humanitarian around."

Bernard V. O'Hare on
Kurt Vonnegut, Jr., in an
unpublished interview, 1973

Slaughterhouse-Five was published in 1969. A short time later, I am told, it was introduced as testimony in the trial of a young man who had destroyed selective-service records—his way of protesting American involvement in the carnage of the war in Vietnam. The defendant, his copy of the novel in hand, testified that he had committed his act of "violence" against the draft system because he could no longer be a Billy Pilgrim. Recall a pertinent scene in the novel: in 1967 Billy Pilgrim listened to the speech of a Marine major who "was in favor of increased bombings, of bombing North Vietnam back into the Stone Age . . . . Billy was not moved to protest the bombing of North Vietnam, did not shudder about the hideous things he himself had seen bombings do. He was simply having lunch with the Lions Club, of which he was past president now."[1]

In 1973 *The Vonnegut Statement* appeared, a collection of articles devoted to the "first, twenty-year phase of Vonnegut's career" and based on the thesis "that *Slaughterhouse-Five* constituted a resolution of

69

sorts to themes and techniques developing throughout his previous work."[2] In his contribution, one of its editors wrote: "Thus, after a tortuous journey through six novels, Vonnegut has finally created a hero who can survive with dignity in an insane world."[3] The "hero" he refers to is the man "simply having lunch with the Lions Club." Clearly, the young man on trial and the critic do not share a common conception of dignity.

Perhaps the young man has read the novel, if simplistically, with more insight and acumen than has the critic, who would evidently like to emulate Billy Pilgrim. Should one find creditable the critic's contentions that Billy has "a deep understanding of the universe," that he has acquired "a vision that enables him to live in this world and yet transcend it at the same . . ., a beatific vision," that he is "a hero both of this world and apart from it" rather than "an anti-hero whose ineffectual acts help no one, not even himself,"[4] then read on: I may be able to provide a new perspective. And I mean "new perspective," not "rebuttal." Though tempted to attack a view of Vonnegut that I find deplorable—one that transforms "the greatest humanitarian around" into a conscienceless escapist—I prefer the indirect method of attempting to solve the intriguing problem posed by the transcendental-hero school of *Slaughterhouse-Five* criticism: what peculiar complexities of the novel, both formal and attitudinal, lead these critics—and I can broaden the field by adding George Roy Hill, the director of the film version—to ecstatic adulation of a well-to-do, middle-aged optometrist who dreams of making "heavenly" love to a sex-symbol movie star on the imaginary planet of Tralfamadore? My solution will suggest that Vonnegut's compassion for Billy Pilgrim's desperate need of "a beatific vision" is not to be mistaken for approval of that vision and its consequences. To comprehend Vonnegut's attitude requires close scrutiny of the demanding complexities of one of the most artistically executed novels in contemporary literature.

THE BIOGRAPHY OF BILLY PILGRIM

The "telegraphic, schizophrenic" form of *Slaughterhouse-Five* makes great demands on even the most sophisticated and acute critics of fiction. But one relatively simple observation opens a door of perception into the novel that can lead to fundamental insights into the technical and thematic subtleties constituting Vonnegut's artistry. That observation is that Vonnegut has taken great care to date precisely various incidents and stages in the life of Billy Pilgrim and just as much care to date the appearances and intrusions of the narrator, who insists on at least a partial identification with Billy and becomes himself a character in the novel. Ultimately this observation leads to the realization that imbedded in the telegraphic, schizophrenic manner of the tale is a considerably detailed biography of Billy Pilgrim and that time-travel, together with the other science-fiction components of the novel, is a brilliant psychological technique devised by Vonnegut to interpret the life and philosophy of his created character.

The dates are there for all to see, if they will: Billy was born in 1922, in 1934 his father took the family on a trip to the Grand Canyon and Carlsbad Caverns, in 1944 Billy was drafted after having started optometry school, in 1948 he had himself committed to a mental institution, in 1957 he was president of the Lions Club, in 1961 he drunkenly tried to commit adultery at a New Year's Eve party, in 1964 he met Kilgore Trout, and so on, these being but a very few of the precisely dated events of his life from birth to his return in 1968 to the practice of optometry after the airplane crash. I omit prebirth ("red light and bubbling sounds"), his "death" on 13 February 1976, and postdeath ("violet light and a hum") simply because they exist only in Billy's imagined "Tralfamadorian life" that, no matter how real to Billy, must be distinguished from his actual life.

Perhaps I attach too much importance to Vonnegut's biographical accuracy, but I have reason to believe that one's comprehension of the meaning and the aesthetic form of the novel may depend to a great extent on the isolation of Billy's biography.

The biographical path will lead, for example, to three corresponding points of time in the lives of Billy and the narrator that must be characterized as deliberate juxtapositions of salient events, functioning as elements of a conscious structural pattern of the novel, designed to signal the distance between the created character Billy and his creator Vonnegut and to alert readers to Vonnegut's critical but—as shall be seen—sympathetic and compassionate evaluation of Billy's response to the cruelty of life.

The first point of time is 1964. In that year Billy was *forced* to remember Dresden; he was not even aware of his inability to remember, so deeply in his subconscious had he buried a memory of Dresden. Vonnegut, too, was unable to remember, but he was aware of that inability and actively sought to overcome it. In 1964, Kurt Vonnegut visited his war buddy Bernard V. O'Hare for the *express purpose of recalling* Dresden. On the telephone Vonnegut said to O'Hare: "I'm writing this book about Dresden. I'd like some help remembering stuff" (p. 4). A few pages on he writes, "A couple of weeks after I telephoned my old war buddy . . ., I really did go to see him. That must have been in 1964 or so . . . " (p. 10).

In 1964, at Billy's wedding-anniversary party,[5] the quartet's singing of "That Old Gang of Mine" aroused in Billy "powerful psychosomatic responses": he could "find no explanation for why the song had affected him so grotesquely. He had supposed for years that he had no secrets from himself. Here was proof that he had a great big secret somewhere inside . . . " (p. 149). Billy did not voluntarily or easily remember Dresden: deeply emotionally racked and desperately in need of relief, Billy "thought hard about the effect the quartet had had on him, and then found an association" (p. 152): four German guards at the Dresden slaughterhouse, emerging after the firestorm, had "looked like a silent film of a barbershop quartet" (p. 153). I quote at length to show that this "secret" memory of Dresden had to be forced into Billy's consciousness. Vonnegut in that same year consciously sought to reinforce his memory of Dresden.

In 1967, the second point of time, Vonnegut's attempt to remember Dresden actually took him back to that city, whereas in 1967 Billy was kidnapped by a flying saucer and taken to Tralfamadore, "he says." More precisely, he escaped to a "planet" created in his own imagination in order to avoid his human responsibilities as surely as Vonnegut, together with O'Hare, in 1967 traveled on this real planet Earth to Dresden in an act of human responsibility.[6] Vonnegut *did* look back when Billy was looking away, and I love Vonnegut for that because it was so human. As he implies by quoting from Roethke's "The Waking" (he had taken a volume of Roethke's poems along to read on the plane to Dresden), he learned by going where he had to go (p. 18). Of course, Billy, too, "had to go" to Tralfamadore, had to create that Eden-like paradise; but he did not learn by going. On the contrary, as shall be seen, his escape to Tralfamadore is a flight from any possibility of learning the responsibilities of wakeful humanity.

The year 1968 is the climactic year: it brings the biography of Billy to its last moment in the narrative present (beyond 1968 there is only Billy's vision of his death in 1976), and it brings Vonnegut to the present moment of writing *Slaughterhouse-Five*; "Robert Kennedy, whose summer home is eight miles from the home I live in all year round, was shot two nights ago. He died last night" (p. 182). The import of the juxtaposition of the creative acts engaged in by Vonnegut and Billy Pilgrim in 1968 seems clear: Vonnegut is writing a novel that rejects the Tralfamadorian philosophy while Billy is actively disseminating that philosophy, first preaching it orally on the all-night radio program and then by writing letters to the Ilium *News Leader*. The chronological correspondence works out with highly suggestive accuracy. How long it takes one to recuperate from a fractured skill, I do not know and the narrator does not say; but he does reveal that "When Billy finally got home to Ilium after the airplane crash [it crashed early in 1968], he was quiet for a while." "And then," the narrator says, "without any warning Billy went to New York City, and got on an all-night radio program." After that, "Another month went by without incident, and then Billy wrote a letter to the Ilium *News Leader* . . ." (p. 22). Surely this passage of time puts Billy's act of writing very close to Vonnegut's act of writing the day after Robert Kennedy's death on June 6.

And what did Billy write? In his second letter to the newspaper, he said, "The most important thing I learned on Tralfamadore was that when a person dies he only *appears* to die" (p. 23). On the morning after writing that letter, Billy went back to work; and in the last moment of the narrative present, which coincides with Vonnegut's comment on the present moment—"And every day my Government gives me a count of corpses created by military science in Vietnam'' (p. 182)—Billy is seen examining the eyes of a boy whose father is a corpse created by military science in Vietnam:

> While he examined the boy's eyes, Billy told him matter-of-factly about his adventures on Tralfamadore, assured the *fatherless* boy that his father was very much alive in moments the boy would see again and again [italics added].
> "Isn't that comforting?" Billy asked. (p. 117)

Billy's total incapacity to understand the significance of the death of human beings clearly distances him from Vonnegut. In effect, Vonnegut says in answer to Barbara's question—"Father, Father, Father—what *are* we going to *do* with you?" (p. 117)—that nothing *can* be done with Billy. The events of 1964, 1967, and 1968 clearly reveal Billy's gradual withdrawal from the human community, a withdrawal that the narrator records with compassion, but as well with censure, as his radically different engagement in life in those years suggests.

The reasons why Billy Pilgrim withdraws from humanity are clearly implicit in his isolable biography. In it, one can trace his indoctrination to the cruelty of the world and discover that his withdrawal from humanity was virtually complete well *before* Billy witnessed the firebombing of Dresden. As emotionally wounding as the Dresden holocaust may have been to Billy, it served largely to confirm a conception of life and death already a part of his being. As the narrator comments on Billy's going crazy in 1948, Eliot Rosewater and he "had both found life meaningless, partly because of what they had seen in war" (p. 87). Only "partly": the major reason, for Billy at least, was discerned by the doctors at the veterans' hospital:

> They didn't think [his going crazy] had anything to do with the war. They were sure Billy was going to pieces because his father had thrown him into the deep end of the Y.M.C.A. swimming pool when he was a little boy, and had then taken him to the rim of the Grand Canyon. (p. 86)

If to the doctors' evidence are added other traumatic childhood experiences, one wonders why Billy had not gone to pieces long before 1948.

He had been "alarmed by the outside world" nearly since birth, and his reason for covering his head when his mother visited him at the veterans' hospital is a condition he suffered from long before his war experiences:

> She made him feel embarrassed and ungrateful and weak because she had gone to so much trouble to give him life, and to keep that life going, and Billy *didn't really like life at all*." (Italics added, p. 88)

With one apparent exception, the childhood experiences of Billy selected by the narrator for mention show why he has never liked life at all; and even that exception turns out not to be an exception, even though it was a pleasant experience. In one of his "time-travels," Billy

> zoomed back in time to his infancy. He was a baby who had just been bathed by his mother. Now his mother wrapped him in a towel, carried him into a rosy room that was filled with sunshine. She unwrapped him, laid him on a tickling towel, powdered him between his legs, joked with him, patted his little jelly belly. Her palm on his little jelly belly made potching sounds.
> Billy gurgled and cooed. (p. 73)

A very pleasant experience, indeed. But if it is contrasted with an unpleasant experience in Billy's sixteenth year, one can see that, since he can not remain a baby gurgling and cooing in response to delightful sensory impressions, it would make him dislike adult life intensely. When at sixteen he visited a doctor, the only patient in the waiting room was "an old, old man" who made sounds far different from gurgling and cooing. He "was in agony because of gas" and he "farted tremendously, and then he belched . . . . 'Oh God'—he said, 'I knew it was going to be bad getting old . . . . I didn't know it was going to be *this* bad' " (p. 163). Billy's eventual creation of Tralfamadore and his life there in a geodesic womb 446,120,000,000,000,000 miles from Earth is in part traceable to his desire to regain his infancy and to escape the old age and death awaiting him in this world.

But the tone of his childhood is better set by a gift given to Billy by his mother in his twelfth year, 1934, a horribly gruesome crucifix she had bought on the trip to the Grand Canyon and Carlsbad Caverns, a purchase made in her attempt "to construct a life that made sense from things she found in gift shops.'' She constructed for Billy a life that made sense, all right, a sense that drove him away from life: "Billy . . . had contemplated torture and hideous wounds at the beginning and the end of nearly every day of his childhood'' (p. 33).

But even earlier, as the doctors correctly surmised, Billy had experienced horror that made him dislike life. In addition to his father's terrifying executionlike throwing of the little Billy into the Y.M.C.A. pool to sink or swim—Billy "dimly sensed that someone was rescuing him. Billy resented that'' (p. 38)—and the visit to the Grand Canyon, also executionlike—"He was sure he was going to fall in. His mother touched him, and he wet his pants'' (p. 77)—there is one other childhood trauma that the doctors did not mention, the visit on the same Western trip when Billy was twelve to the Carlsbad Caverns: "Billy was praying to God to get him out of there before the ceiling fell in.'' Rather than get him out of there, God subjected him to further trauma: the ranger turned out the lights and plunged Billy into "darkness that was total . . . . Billy didn't even know whether he was still alive or not'' (p. 77).

Yes, the doctors are right. Though in the narrative sequence Billy's—and the doctors'—belief that he is going crazy does not surface until 1948, even at the age of twelve, in 1934, Billy had undergone the real crises of his life, had found life meaningless even if he could not then articulate that concept, and was in desperate need of reinventing himself and his universe. Vonnegut's biographical exposition of Billy's formative years implies that Billy was at twelve already well on his way to Tralfamadore. Here is the true time-travel of the novel: a linear, chronological development clearly based on a cause-and-effect relationship. The child is indeed the father of the man who searches for a prelapsarian Eden. And readers are in the presence, not of science fiction, but of profound satirical fiction probing the condition of modern man.

A brief examination of the implications of Billy's formative years shows that although Vonnegut is intensely concerned about World War II and the Vietnamese War, the novel transcends any specific events of our time. Vonnegut's ultimate concern is to question the origin and the viability of the myths man lives by and finally to reject any new lie that deprives man of his dignity and his life of significance. In this sense, *Slaughterhouse-Five* is a profoundly religious novel.

The religious-mythical significance of the novel emerges in an analysis of the events of Billy's formative years. In the figure of his own father Billy has experienced the cruel tyranny of The God of This Universe and has learned to hate life in this Universe. The meaning of the gruesome crucifix—"Christ died horribly"—is clear: one Father subjected his Son to a horrible death and rendered Him pitiful (p. 33). The cruel sink-or-swim method Billy's father used to teach Billy how to survive in lifegiving water is a grotesque rite of baptism: Vonnegut identifies the water as the Y.M. C(hristian) A. pool. At the Grand Canyon, where his father kicks a pebble to the floor of the canyon, "one mile straight down," and pronounces, "Well..., there it is," like God announcing his creation, the family stands on Bright Angel Point. And Billy's father terrifies him just as much in the hell of Carlsbad Caverns as he did in the heaven of Grand Canyon: Billy prayed to God to get him out of the cavern and instead was plunged into total darkness that made him doubt his existence. The only "ghostly" light points to the person responsible for his terror: "His father had taken out his pocket watch. The watch had a radium dial" (p. 77). To be told that the Supreme Ruler of the Universe is the Utterly Indifferent God is one thing: it is another to experience at first hand as an impressionable child the depraved, or, at best, insensitive cruelty of a living god who should protect, comfort, and guide. If at twelve or at twenty-one Billy had had the wisdom of a Bokonon and had ice-nine been within reach, he would have turned himself into ice, lying on his back and thumbing his nose at You Know Who.

SCIENCE FICTION TRANSLATED INTO REALISTIC-PSYCHOLOGICAL FICTION

Billy is destined never to achieve the wisdom of Bokonon, though the means he devised to cope with a universe ruled by the Utterly Indifferent God result in a spiritual death as absolute as the physical death caused by ice-nine. To continue to trace Billy's biography, particularly from his coming of age in 1944, through his war experiences, to his return home after the war, involves necessarily a direct examination of those means; for it is at this point in the chronological sequence of Billy's life that

Vonnegut introduces the two dominant science-fiction elements of the novel—Tralfamadore and time-travel—the products of Billy's imagination that constitute the illusory means he devises in order to survive. To distinguish the true from the fanciful, the authentic facts of the life of Billy from the products of his imagination, is essential. Vonnegut insists that readers make that distinction, as can be seen when one pays attention to the narrative mode of the novel. "Listen!" Vonnegut often says. One must listen very carefully to how he is telling the story of Billy Pilgrim.

Although the narrator often clearly differentiates time-travel and hallucination—for example, at one point he writes, "Billy Pilgrim was having a delightful hallucination.... This wasn't time-travel" (p. 42)—the carefully controlled narrative voice leaves no doubt that Billy imagines his time-traveling as surely as he imagines Tralfamadore. The beginning of the narrative proper at the opening of chapter 2 supplies the evidence that compels the reader to distinguish between the true and the imagined in Billy's life. The first words of that chapter—"Listen: Billy Pilgrim has come unstuck in time" (p. 20)—are followed by a brief paragraph summarizing his erratic wanderings in time, and that paragraph includes a clear attribution of the summary to Billy: "he says." Then in a sharply isolated paragraph, resounding in its emphasis, the attribution is repeated:

He says.

Again it is repeated in the next brief paragraph that records Billy's attitude toward being "spastic in time." But the next sentence—"Billy was born in 1922 in Illium, New York... "—begins a one-and-a-half page biographical synopsis of the actual facts of Billy's life up to his appearance in 1968 on the all-night radio program. The attribution to Billy does not appear at all *until* the narrator refers *again* to time-travel and Tralfamadore: "*He told* about having come unstuck in time. *He said*, too, that he had been kidnapped by a flying saucer in 1967" (italics added, p. 22). And thereafter in the synopsis the attribution appears only when the narrator refers to Billy's beliefs about time-travel and Tralfamadore.

Do I belabor an obvious point? An editor of *The Vonnegut Statement* does not think it obvious at all, for one thing[7]; and I need clearly to establish the distinction between the real and the imagined in Billy's life in order to show that the true import of *Slaughterhouse-Five*, in all of its complexity, can not be grasped without painstaking and sensitive appraisal of the stuff of which Billy's imagination is made. To engage in that appraisal is, after all, to respond to the integral narrative technique of the novel.

The first painstaking job, then, is to trace the evolution of Tralfamadore in Billy Pilgrim's mind; in this labor one should discover the profound psychic needs that Billy satisfies by creating Tralfamadore and inventing time-travel.

Billy's creation of Tralfamadore is his response to a challenge that he overheard Eliot Rosewater make to a psychiatrist in the veterans' hospital: "I think you guys are going to have to come up with a lot of wonderful *new* lies, or people just aren't going to want to go on living" (pp. 87-88). The source of the new lies that Billy comes up with is hinted by the narrator when he comments of both Eliot and Billy, " . . . they were trying to reinvent themselves and their universe. *Science fiction was a big help*" (italics added, p. 87). Without science fiction Billy could not have succeeded. His new lies and his new universe were created out of novels used as window dressing in a porno shop, the science fiction of Kilgore Trout.

The stimuli to Billy's imagination lay in a trunk of science-fiction paperbacks under Eliot Rosewater's bed in that veterans' hospital in 1948: "It was Rosewater who introduced Billy to science fiction, and in particular to the writings of Kilgore Trout" (p. 87). Tralfamadore itself and Billy's and Montana Wildhack's display in a ''zoo'' there originated in 1948 when Billy read in the hospital a Trout novel called *The Big Board*:

> It was about an Earthling man and woman who were kidnapped by extra-terrestrials. They were put on display in a zoo on a planet called Zircon 212. (p. 174)

In addition, Trout's novel supplied Billy with some ''Tralfamadorian'' ideas and even with the mode by which his imagination would transport him and Montana to Tralfamadore:

> On Tralfamadore, says Billy Pilgrim, there isn't much interest in

Jesus Christ. The Earthling figure who is most engaging to the Tral-
famadorian mind, he says, is Charles Darwin—who taught that those
who die are meant to die, that corpses are improvements . . . .
   The same general idea appears in *The Big Board* by Kilgore Trout.
The flying saucer creatures who capture Trout's hero ask him about
Darwin. (p. 182)

Here is the origin of Billy's conception of death, though the Zircon 212
Darwinism that he has translated in his imagination into the Tralfama
dorian attitude toward death was certainly reinforced by his own observation of death in World War II.

   The same pattern of stimulation to Billy's imagination—life col-
laborating with science fiction—can be discerned in the reference to the
Tralfamadorians' (Billy's) lack of interest in Christ. Because of the
childhood impression made by the gruesome crucifix in his room—
"Billy's Christ died horribly" (p. 33)—Billy was ready to take to heart
the message of another Trout novel wherein a time-traveler listened with
a stethoscope to the body of Christ on the cross: "There wasn't a
sound . . . . The Son of God was dead as a doornail" (p. 176).

   Obviously, too, that novel and others by Trout are the origins of Billy's
belief in time-traveling: "Most of Trout's novels . . . dealt with time
warps and extrasensory perception and other unexpected things" (p.
150). In addition to time-travel, one of those "unexpected things" is the
conception of the reality of the fourth dimension that Billy attributes to
the Tralfamadorians. It is traceable to Trout's *Maniacs in the Fourth
Dimension*:

   One thing Trout said . . . was that there really *were* vampires and
   werewolves and goblins and angels and so on, but that they were in the
   fourth dimension. (p. 90)

Billy's daughter Barbara is at least partly correct in the assumption she
expresses in reaction to Billy's radio talk and letters about Tralfamadore:

   "You know who I could just kill?" she asked.
   "*Who* could you kill?" said Billy.
   "That Kilgore Trout." (p. 142)

But Barbara only knows that Billy has been reading Trout's novels; she
can not read his mind. As I suggested earlier, Trout's novels are only

partly responsible for the creations of Billy's imagination: his own experiences in life and especially his desire to escape from a world that he can not cope with animate the imagination stimulated by Trout's fiction. The origin of Montana Wildhack as Billy's mate on Tralfamadore is a good illustration.

Trout's *The Big Board* supplied the outline—"an Earthling man and woman . . . on display in a zoo"—but the substance of Billy's vision of Montana is the creation of both the tawdriest and most profound forces of Billy's psyche. As proved by the *old* girly magazine whose cover question, "What really became of Montana Wildhack?", Billy reads in 1968, Montana actually is a filmstar who had disappeared some time before 1968. Billy says of his mate on Tralfamadore, "The last thing she remembered was sunning herself by a swimming pool in Palm Springs, California" (p. 115); but who knows what *really* became of Montana? Billy does not, but the disappearance of a voluptuous sex queen has triggered his made-in-Hollywood fantasies, and his imagination provides for his Tralfamadorian bed the young and beautiful mate who can fulfill the sexual dreams he denied himself by taking as his real mate the fat and ugly Valencia.

But Montana only incidentally fulfills Billy's sexual fantasies. As the Eve in his created Eden of Tralfamadore, she is the fulfillment of the mythical-paradisiacal alternative to the world he can not cope with, an alternative that has been his dream for a long time. In 1944, lying on the ice and staring into the golden patina of the boots worn by the German corporal who had captured him, Billy "saw Adam and Eve in the golden depths. They were naked. They were so innocent, so vulnerable, so eager to behave decently. Billy Pilgrim loved them" (p. 46). And in 1967 when he sees the television war movie backwards, Billy extrapolates, his edenic dream carrying him well beyond the limits of the film: "Everybody turned into a baby, and all humanity, without exception, conspired biologically to produce two perfect people named Adam and Eve . . . " (pp. 64-65). Clearly, in his imagined Tralfamadore Billy has made his edenic dream come true: he has transfigured his forty-six-year-old self and the twenty-year-old Montana into naked, innocent, decently behaving perfect people in a geodesic Eden far from a life and a world he never liked.

One vital question about Billy's creation of Tralfamadore remains:

when did the vision of Tralfamadore form in his mind? Because of the telegraphic, schizophrenic manner of the tale, it is a difficult question to answer. *Billy says* that he first traveled in time in 1944, and in his fifth time-travel (occurring on Christmas night of 1944 in the prisoners' boxcar) he "traveled in time to 1967 . . . —to the night he was kidnapped by a flying saucer from Tralfamadore" (p. 61). Yet he did not read until 1948 the Trout novels out of which he created Tralfamadore. The resolution of this apparent discrepancy is essential since one can not understand the psychological function of time-travel without knowing when Billy actually first "traveled in time" to Tralfamadore, that is, when he first conceived of Tralfamadore in his imagination.

Feeding on Vonnegut's clues, I put the time early in 1968, precisely on the day when Valencia was being buried and Billy, his skull fractured, lay conscious in his hospital bed, outwardly listless: "The listlessness concealed a mind which was fizzing and flashing thrillingly. It was preparing letters and lectures about the flying saucers, the negligibility of death, and the nature of time" (p. 164). Although the reference to "letters and lectures" suggests that Billy was planning to share with the world a vision already formed, Vonnegut supports the speculation that it was at this very moment that Billy is experiencing the thrill of creating that vision: the narrator insists that Billy *never* spoke of Tralfamadore until *after* this day. About a scene in 1965 the narrator comments: "This was before Billy had his head broken in an airplane crash, by the way—before he became so vocal about flying saucers and traveling in time" (p. 39). When Barbara asks, "Why is it that you never mentioned any of this before the airplane crash?", Billy's answer—"I didn't think the time was ripe" (p. 26)— merits skepticism. In the clearly traceable time sequence of the narrative, the first person he ever mentions Tralfamadore to is not Kilgore Trout, as might be expected since Trout would have surely lent a receptive and sympathetic ear, but Professor Rumfoord during their discussion of Dresden (p. 171), after the mind in that broken head had fizzed and flashed brilliantly.

Besides, Vonnegut mentions someone else with a fractured skull, apparently planting a correspondence that may be the most conclusive evidence that Tralfamadore was conceived in Billy's broken head. Of the two books that Vonnegut planned to read on his journey to Dresden in

1967, the thematic relevance of one has already been suggested. Vonnegut's pointed comments on the other—Erika Ostrovsky's *Céline and His Vision*—establish an intriguing, ironic comparison between Céline and Billy. After his skull fracture, Céline became a doctor and treated poor people; the optometrist Billy began to prescribe "corrective lenses for Earthling souls . . ., lost and wretched" (p. 25). Of Céline Vonnegut pointedly remarks, "Time obsessed him" (p. 18); Billy is also obsessed with time. But the most pertinent aspect of the ironic comparison is the correspondence of Billy's attitude and that of Céline in his novel *Death on the Installment Plan*. Recall Billy's concept of "death on the installment plan," his assurances to "the fatherless boy that his father was very much alive in moments the boy would see again and again." In the novel, Vonnegut relates, Céline

> screams on paper, *Make them stop . . . don't let them move anymore at all . . . . There, make them freeze . . . once and for all! . . . So that they won't disappear anymore!* (p. 19)

"So that they won't disappear anymore"—is not that the purpose of Billy's ardent belief in the Tralfamadorian conception of immortality, "when a person dies he only appears to die"?

Another discrimination between Céline and Billy, it seems to me, gives insight into Vonnegut's subtly satirical commentary on the imagination at work in Billy's broken head. Céline, Vonnegut reveals, wrote that "no art is possible without a dance with death" and came to the ultimate conclusion that "*The truth is death*" (p. 18). No art is possible for Billy because he can not dance with death, can not face the truth. Rather, his imagination carries him back to the mythical childhood of mankind, to a prelapsarian edenic paradise that knows no death, and shields him from reality with a Tralfamadorian doctrine that denies the truth of death.

Do not misconstrue my intention. *Slaughterhouse-Five* would be meaningless should one dismiss Billy's creation of Tralfamadore as a sign of insanity. On the contrary, Tralfamadore makes very good sense, given the absurdity of the real world; and the deterministic Tralfamadorian philosophy is founded on undeniable truths, as shall be seen. I want to show only that Tralfamadore and its philosophy, together with time-travel, came into play in 1968, only a few months before the life story of Billy Pilgrim is brought to its conclusion in the narrative present. In other words, having isolated the actual biography of Billy Pilgrim, one can see that the science-fiction elaboration of that story is Billy's post-crash transformation of his actual life into a version that enables him to justify every moral failure of his life, to silence his conscience, to free him of all responsibility, to escape reality. In sum, in 1968 he reinvents himself and his universe.

Time-travel, in particular the ability to foretell the future that it entails, is the means that Billy evolves from science-fiction sources to make bearable sense of his life. Consider Billy's reaction to his two traumatic war experiences, the bombing of Dresden and the execution of Edgar Derby. To the death of Edgar Derby Billy is totally indifferent; neither at the time nor later does he show any emotional response whatsoever to Derby's death. He speaks of Derby, true, but always objectively and matter-of-factly. His inability to respond to the death of the man who befriended him is one of the unbearable truths about himself that he must live with until he can find a justification for his attitude and silence his conscience, just as he must try to cope with the incomprehensible, arbitrary cruelty of a world in which the wanton destruction of a city that was to him like heaven and the senseless slaughter of 135,000 innocent people can occur. Time-travel enables Billy to accept a world beyond comprehension and to relieve himself of all sense of guilt.

Billy's belief that he has freedom in time and can foresee the future is actually a very common psychological defense mechanism, essentially a matter of rationalizing after the fact, of inventing good excuses for not doing or reacting as one ought. Vonnegut's phrasing clearly alerts one to the psychological function of time-travel:

> Billy, with his memories of the future, knew that the city would be smashed to smithereens and then burned—in about thirty more days. He knew, too, that most of the people watching him would soon be dead. (p. 131)

The key word is *memories*. Although Vonnegut does not explicitly attribute the vision of a future event to Billy by use of the formula "he says," the word *memories* clearly implies that Vonnegut is referring to

Billy's reconstruction in 1968 of his past life. One has memories of the past, not of the future; and in 1968 Billy does have memories of the Dresden bombing. What he does is to convince himself in 1968 that he really did foresee the destruction of Dresden: his memory of the past confirms that it happened *just as he foresaw it*. The moment was so structured. It is futile to concern oneself about events that had to happen, he rationalizes.

Similarly Billy absolves himself of guilt and quiets his conscience for being indifferent to the death of Edgar Derby. In 1968 Billy believes that in 1944 he

> saw in his memory of the future poor old Edgar Derby in front of a firing squad in the ruins of Dresden. There were only four men in that squad. Billy had heard that one man in each firing squad was customarily given a rifle loaded with [a] blank cartridge. Billy didn't think there would be a blank cartridge issued in a squad that small, in a war that old. (pp. 90-91)

Since Billy is recalling a fact—Derby was shot to death by a four-man squad—his belief that he foresaw the execution excuses his failure to do anything to prevent it. Whether he could have prevented it had he tried is beside the point. He assures himself that the execution happened just as it had to happen and thus assuages his guilt for not having cared about the death of Derby: one ought to be indifferent to an unalterable fact, he rationalizes. This process of rationalization is clearly implied in the phrasing of Billy's "memory of the future": noting from memory that Derby was shot to death, he has dismissed that fact and allowed his mind to wander to thoughts about the firing squad.

It can not be an accidental effect of the erratic narrative pattern that the paragraph following Billy's "memory of the future" execution of Derby aptly characterizes Billy's attitude toward Derby and the destruction of Dresden. The English officer who had given Billy morphine asks Derby,

> "How's the patient?"
> "Dead to the world."
> "But not actually dead."
> "No."

"How nice—to feel nothing, and still get full credit for being alive." (p. 91)

The psychological function of Billy's travels in time is to allow him "to feel nothing" and yet give himself "full credit for being alive."

Significantly, Billy depends on the same function and the same effects when he imagines time-travel to his death: "As a time-traveler, he has seen his own death many times . . ." (pp. 122-23). In recording Billy's "foretelling" of his death, Vonnegut provides clear evidence that imagined time-travel enables Billy to construct a comforting version of his known past; for Vonnegut shows Billy's imagination at work in precisely the same way on the unknown future. Just as time-travel allows Billy passively to accept events that were beyond his control, to excuse his failure to act on or respond to events within his control, and to assuage his conscience, so, too, does it allow him to accept that future event beyond anyone's control—death—and to justify his indifference toward it. Assured that he will die on 13 February 1976, Billy provides a vividly detailed account of the event. The horrors of the past have been projected into the future: Dresden has become hydrogen-bombed Chicago, reflecting Billy's fatalistic conviction that nothing can be done to prevent senseless slaughter. The agent of his death is Paul Lazzaro, whose actual threat against his life in 1944 Billy will see fulfilled, reflecting his equally fatalistic conviction that what will happen has to happen, that it is futile to try to avoid the "structured moment." And he will be just another Edgar Derby, since he cares no more about his own death than he did about the death of Derby. Comforted by his Tralfamadorian doctrine of immortality—"it is time for me to be dead for a little while—and then live again" (p. 124)—he has imagined for himself a death that he need not fear or even bother his mind about: death will be another painless, trivial event of his life, he rationalizes. Time-travel has again enabled Billy to escape the truth, this time the truth of death. Yes, science fiction was for Billy a big help indeed.

THE DIVIDED SELVES OF VONNEGUT
DISCOVERED IN THE NARRATIVE MODE

To this point, the analysis of the telegraphic, schizophrenic manner of

Slaughterhouse-Five has been almost exclusively concentrated on the created character Billy Pilgrim. I have described a schizophrenia of sorts in Billy's inability to distinguish reality from illusion, in his invention of another self and another universe that allows him to live in this world and yet apart from it. And the telegraphic manner of the tale I have attributed to Billy's erratic traveling in time: Vonnegut has so structured the story that the reader must experience an erratic narrative lacking in the expected chronological sequence in order to come to understand the psychological, imaginative life of a character who can not bear to face his actual life.

But there is another telegraphic, schizophrenic dimension to *Slaughterhouse-Five* that must be explored if readers are to grasp the full complexity and ultimate import of the novel. I speak of the narrative mode of the novel, particularly Vonnegut's adoption of a variety of narrative voices. The narrative is telegraphic in the sense that Vonnegut's various narrative voices send several messages, each in its distinct tone, and the job as responsible readers is to discover why and to what effect he indulges in this complex mode. Ultimately one discovers that the narrative mode is schizophrenic, that the sender of the messages is a divided self whose psychic conflict forces him to communicate with others from the opposed poles of his psyche. To analyze the narrative mode of the novel is to analyze its primary subject—its author.

Already I have indirectly isolated two narrative voices: a third-person-omniscient narrator who tells Billy's actual life story and an objective reportorial narrator who records Billy's imaginative life as Billy "has told" it to the narrator. But other voices are heard, most notably the first-person voice of chapters 1 and 10 that readers are apparently expected to take as the actual voice of the author, and the intrusive first-person voice that at four points in the narrative interjects the exclamation "I was there." The effect of two of the four intrusions is to introduce the "author" into the story as a character whose actions are recorded in the third person by the omniscient narrator. For example:

> An American near Billy wailed that he had excreted everything but his brains. Moments later he said, "There they go, there they go." He meant his brains.
> That was I. That was me. That was the author of this book. (p. 109)[8]

Yet another narrative voice can be detected: an authorial, editorial voice occasionally commenting on Billy. For example:

> Which is why the epigraph of this book is the quatrain from the famous Christmas carol. Billy cried very little, though he often saw things worth crying about, and in *that* respect, at least, he resembled the Christ of the carol . . . . (p. 170)

Given its touch of satirical tone, this bit of editorializing has to be distinguished from the omniscient narrator's nonsatirical observations, like

> Every so often, for no apparent reason, Billy Pilgrim would find himself weeping. Nobody had ever caught Billy doing it. Only the doctor knew. (p. 53)

In addition to these narrative voices, a "presence" is felt throughout the novel, a pervading artistic presence to whom one must attribute the structural patterns—some quite subtle, others insistent—that because of their pervasiveness and significance make one aware of a controlling hand forming the whole of the novel. I refer not only to the recurring imagery of "nestling like spoons," ivory and blue, orange and black, radium, mustard gas and roses, and so on, but also to various ironic juxtapositions—the components of which are often widely separated in the text—like the recurrence of references to the Children's Crusade, to the Three Musketeers, and to revenge as a motive for the bombing of Dresden (Paul Lazarro and Harry Truman). Ultimately the impression generated by this hard-to-define presence is that in this apparently erratic, even eccentric novel, nothing is extraneous, whimsical, or disconnected: every element is essential and is in its proper place. Readers can not doubt that they are experiencing a work of art, that the artist never wants them to forget that they are encountering a carefully wrought object that only superficially appears to be "jumbled and jangled." Vonnegut has informed the whole with an artistic presence that constitutes a subtly dominant element of the narrative mode.

All of these voices are Kurt Vonnegut's, yet each has a discrete function. Kurt Vonnegut-novelist has created in Billy Pilgrim a fictional character whose biographically detailed life from 1922 to mid-1968 the omniscient narrator records. This "true" history concludes at that point (p. 117) when Billy's daughter Barbara takes him home following his attempt to comfort the boy whose father was killed in Vietnam. The objective, reportorial narrator records the science-fiction life that Billy believes he has lived. By attributing the imagined life of time-travel and Tralfamadore to Billy—"He says"—this narrative voice is a means of carefully distinguishing the imagined from the actual life of Billy. Thus these two third-person narrative voices function to establish Billy's schizophrenia. Simultaneously, they permit the novelist-Vonnegut to so structure the narrative that readers are forced to experience the imagined, illusory life of his created character, to travel erratically in time with Billy and to be shunted from Earth to Tralfamadore with him so that they will come to understand Billy's state of mind as well as the conditions that produced it.

The effect of the first-person voices, one of which introduces the first person into the narrative as a character, is to establish the complex relationship between the created character and the novelist, complex in that it both associates and dissociates Billy and Vonnegut. By intruding into the narrative ("I was there") the novelist associates himself with Billy by suggesting that he underwent virtually the same experiences as Billy's from his arrival on the battle front to the end of the war.[9] Otherwise, biographically, the two lives are quite distinct: as the novelist relates in chapter 1, while Billy was going to optometry school and later while making a bundle as an optometrist in Ilium, Vonnegut was a reporter in Chicago, a student of anthropology at the University of Chicago, a public-relations man for General Electric in Schenectady, and then a writer on Cape Cod, and so forth.

Yet the artistic presence makes me aware that as vastly different as Billy's and Vonnegut's lives have been—the war years being an exception—Billy and Vonnegut are not to be entirely dissociated. An intimate, spiritual kinship of the two is implied in occasional touches of imagery and in unmistakable juxtapositions. When Vonnegut visited O'Hare in 1964, he carried a "bottle of Irish whiskey like a dinner bell" (p. 11); on the night of his daughter's wedding, Billy carried a champagne bottle, "swinging the bottle like a dinner bell" (p. 63). On that same night in 1967, Vonnegut, the drunk with breath like mustard gas and roses who has a habit of calling old friends on the phone late at night, makes contact with Billy. Though the narrator says, "It was a wrong number," a drunk *was* on the other end: "Billy could almost smell his breath—mustard gas and roses" (p. 63). It *was* Vonnegut, of course, trying to make contact with Billy, to bring to him their shared memory of the rotted and liquified bodies of Dresdeners that stank like roses and mustard gas. Vonnegut was trying to get in touch with his spiritual kin, with the self within that wants to withdraw from life, from its horrors and its responsibilities, to fly with Billy to Tralfamadore, where life is guilt free. When at another time a crazy thought occurs to Billy—"Everything was beautiful, and nothing hurt" (p. 106)—Vonnegut intrudes in the first person to confirm what is elsewhere implied, that he is associated with and shares Billy's psychic life: "It would make a good epitaph for Billy Pilgrim, and for me, too" (p. 105).

Clearly, Vonnegut participates spiritually in the imaginative life generated from Billy's psychic needs. The objective narrator reporting what "Billy says" is giving expression to Vonnegut's own *Billy Pilgrim-self.* Readers have to translate "he says" into "my Billy Pilgrim-self says," for in recording Billy's escape from the tyranny of sequential time and from this world to the edenic paradise of Tralfamadore, Vonnegut is projecting that pole of a divided psyche that is compellingly attracted to a guilt-free determinism that can acquit him of all concern and responsibility, free him from his own history and that of mankind, and allow him to sink softly into the oblivion of infant innocence.

Vonnegut's schizophrenia is thus reflected in the distinction between the major narrative voices in which he speaks. But the other narrative voices reveal that Vonnegut does exercise a strength of will that keeps his Billy Pilgrim-self in check. In various ways, the first-person voice of chapters 1 and 10, the editorial voice, and, ultimately of the greatest import, the artistic presence reveal that Vonnegut the novelist and man maintains a critical sensitivity to the aberrations and fatuities of his Billy Pilgrim-self that preserves his psychic health. To examine the satirical tone and techniques of the novel is to discover both how the voices of the narrative mode convey that critical sensitivity and what crucial deficiencies in Billy Pilgrim's Tralfamadorian solution to his cosmic plight keep Vonnegut from adopting the same solution.

IDENTIFICATION OF THE SATIRICAL
AND THE SATIRISTS

The first-person voice of chapter 10 makes a comment that strikes precisely the note to alert the reader to the satirical tone of the novelist's treatment of Billy Pilgrim's Tralfamadorianism:

> If what Billy learned from the Tralfamadorians is true, that we will all live forever, no matter how dead we may sometimes seem to be, I am not overjoyed. (pp. 182-83)

What he learned is put in a different way by Billy himself in his letter to the Ilium *News Leader*, put in a way that raises a fundamental crux of the novel:

> when I myself hear that somebody is dead, I simply shrug and say what the Tralfamadorians say about dead people, which is "So it goes." (p. 23)

Since it is the *narrator* who applies the phrase "So it goes" after each mention of death, even in the first and last chapters where the narrative voice is most clearly the actual voice of Vonnegut, does Vonnegut share Billy's Tralfamadorian attitude toward death, even if he says he is not overjoyed by the Tralfamadorian conception of immortality?

Vonnegut's carefully toned "I am not overjoyed" has to be considered the ironic understatement of the novel when one catches the satirical effect of the constant reiteration of the phrase "So it goes." One can hardly conceive of an apter phrase to encapsulate the Tralfamadorian indifference to death. Properly alerted to the significance of its constant reiteration, readers can hardly fail to miss Vonnegut's intensely satirical denunciation of that attitude toward death.

A close look at each context in which "So it goes" is applied reveals a satirical technique not much different in effect from Alexander Pope's brilliant anticlimaxes. In toto, its use constitutes a deliberate, ironic juxtaposition in the manner of Pope: a carefully structured distortion of values designed to alert readers to Vonnegut's disapproval of the values manifested in the Tralfamadorian belief that death is inconsequential.

Ordering those contexts according to a descending scale reveals what the satirist Vonnegut is really saying.

Like Billy in his letter, the narrator applies the phrase "So it goes" to the mention of the deaths of human beings, most notably the deaths of 135,000 Dresdeners, and Edgar Derby, *and* Lucretia A. Mott, the suffragette whose name is borne by the freighter on which Billy was shipped home from Europe, *and* murder victims on television shows, *and* "the picture of one cowboy killing another one pasted to the television tube" on Tralfamadore (no place). "So it goes" also follows the mention of fictional death in other contexts: Trout's people who killed themselves around the money tree and—not to mention everyone in Trout's fiction—the French chef on whose body in the casket mourners sprinkled parsley and paprika. And it is applied to the deaths of animals, real and fictional, with just as much diligence: three times to the dead animals of Germany—"killed and eaten and excreted by human beings" (p. 132)— to Billy's dog Spot, and to a hypothetical dog—if Lazarro had been a dog, says the narrator, he would have been shot and his head sent to a laboratory, "to see if he had rabies. So it goes" (p. 125). From animals, the narrator descends the Great Chain of Being to body lice and bacteria—"dying by the billions. So it goes" (p. 73)—and then abandons the Chain of Being altogether to Tralfamadorize a lowly glass of water—"The water was dead. So it goes" (p. 88)—and an elite half-bottle of champagne. Like the 135,000 human beings of Dresden, "The champagne was dead. So it goes" (p. 63).

This juxtaposition can be nothing but the satirist's way of saying that the death of human beings *is* significant, that one can not be indifferent to the value of human life. Surely, then, readers are expected to respond to Vonnegut's incisively critical irony when he speaks of Billy's offering comfort by explaining the Tralfamadorian conception of death to a *"fatherless* boy" (Vonnegut's word, italics added, p. 117).

Similarly, Vonnegut as omnipresent satirist undermines the apparent good sense of other Tralfamadorian concepts and asks readers to see Tralfamadore itself as it really is. Constantly distancing himself—and readers— from Tralfamadorianism by a variety of techniques, Vonnegut forces the reflective reader to see its distortions and perversions of reality. Its cardinal principle and quintessence is subjected to a series of such satirical techniques. The concept that the moment is so structured that it has to happen in a certain way appears in a telling scene, in a conversation between Billy and Montana immediately after she refers to a past moment that Billy has convinced himself had to happen just as it did—the death of Edgar Derby. The narrator continues,

> She moved the baby from one breast to the other, because the moment was so structured that she *had* to do so. (Italics Vonnegut's, p. 179)

The satirical touch is small but sufficient.

In a totally different context, the same touch is evident. Telling the story of the airplane crash, the narrator chooses to mention a triviality and to add a matter-of-fact comment that seems, at first glance, to reflect his serious belief in determinism:

> The plane took off without incident. The moment was structured that way. (p. 133)

Every airplane in the world, from the commencement of flight up to the present, that "took off without incident" did so because the "moment was structured that way." The narrator has clearly implied that determinism is nonsense. Of course, this particular airplane did crash, and by implication every other plane—and car and bicycle and tricycle— that has crashed *had* to. This Determinism is a very busy fellow, indeed, especially since he has to see to every incident in the universe and at the same time tell every mother in the world just when to shift her baby to the other breast.

His deliberate failure to specify what did cause the crash of Billy's plane is Vonnegut's implied reminder that determinism accounts for no responsible human action whatsoever. Is he not implying a similar adverse judgment of determinism when he reports Billy's assertion that the Tralfamadorians do not see human beings as what they are: "And Tralfamadorians don't see human beings as two-legged creatures . . . . They see them as great millipedes—'with babies' legs at one end and old people's legs at the other,' says Billy Pilgrim" (p. 75)? Vonnegut's Billy Pilgrim-self conveys a truth here: human beings *are* fixed in an inexorable progression from infancy to old age to death. But it is "more true" that at each stage men are two-legged creatures and on their two legs they must stand when they act—or fail to act—in response to the daily situations they have to face.

I am reminded of the Houyhnhnms's flawed perception of Gulliver: they see only a Yahoo. Insofar as human beings are Yahoos, their perception is valid; but they do not see the whole man, the animal *and* the rational being. Vonnegut is Swiftian also in the way he casts doubt on the acceptability of the Tralfamadorians and their philosophy. Swift, for instance, has his Houyhnhnms practice a rational control over reproduction impossible for human beings to practice, and he adds touches to his description of Houyhnhnmland that alert readers to his critical attitude: the horses squat on their haunches to eat and a mare threads a needle by holding it between pastern and hoof. Vonnegut's description of Tralfamadore has much the same effect on readers sensitive to the satirical. Not only does their physical appearance raise more than a smile—

> two feet high, and green, and shaped like plumber's friends. Their suction cups were on the ground . . . . At the top of each shaft was a little hand with a green eye in its palm (pp. 22-23)

—their beliefs and perceptions are inherently ridiculous, showing how far removed the little green Tralfamadorians are from the world of human reality: they see in four dimensions and believe that seven sexes are required to produce an Earthling baby; five of the seven sexes are, of course, active only in the fourth dimension. Tralfamadore is, like Houyhnhnmland, conceived in the tradition of the utopia inaccessible to man, that is, not only "no place" but also an antiutopia that no one can inhabit if he is to remain a human being. Tralfamadore is 446,120,000,000,000,000 miles from Earth, and to reach it Billy and Montana travel by "flying saucer" through "time warps," whatever they may be. There they "live" in a geodesic womb, breathing oxygen piped from the cyanide world of the Tralfamadorians.

Billy Pilgrim is cast in the traditional role of the naif whose experiences unfit him for life in the human world, another Gulliver, as it were. Like Gulliver, Billy has been driven to an extreme state of mind approaching insanity. Gulliver's extended painful and shattering educational experiences have left him a raging misanthrope denouncing for all time any association with his "Yahoo" countrymen. His *Travels*, the pride-motivated grand project designed to reform the human race, is his hope of making the world tolerable. Billy Pilgrim has had so many traumatic shocks in his childhood and young manhood that he withdraws from the human world and ultimately conceives of Tralfamadore and its deterministic nihilism as a way of making life tolerable. Preaching the Tralfamadorian philosophy, "prescribing corrective lenses for Earthling souls," as he puts it, is the grand project of his life, though unlike Gulliver's it is motivated by a sincere desire to help his fellow man. And just as Swift distances himself from Gulliver by having him denounce pride in a raging speech rank with Gulliver's own pride, so too does the satirist Vonnegut distance himself from Billy by having him "comfort" a fatherless boy with an explanation of death that can comfort only Billy, who is too far gone in his desperate commitment to deterministic nihilism to recognize his fatuousness, not to speak of the cruelty he inflicts on the boy. Both Gulliver and Billy are victims, overexposed to the worst of life on earth and insufficiently supported by strength of character and an enduring system of human values. Each loses perspective on and ultimately contact with reality. The miseducation of Gulliver has its counterpart in the tragic education of Billy Pilgrim, and neither Swift nor Vonnegut advocates or even approves the extreme state of mind of his central character, though each understands its origins and causes.

This exploration into the satirical dimensions of *Slaughterhouse-Five* leads to other observations that coalesce with earlier observations on the schizophrenic narrative mode. As I stated earlier, the narrative technique projects two Vonneguts into the novel, his Billy Pilgrim-self and a self in opposition to the Pilgrim-self. Further analysis of the satirical techniques reinforces that contention and elaborates upon it: just as there are two selves of Vonnegut, so too are there two satirists. An examination of the personas created by the novelist shows that Vonnegut has indeed projected into the novel his divided self and that each self has its corresponding satirical voice.

The first persona is the satirically functional persona of the kind created by Pope in, for example, "Epistle to Dr. Arbuthnot." The rhetorical practice consists in the satirist's attributing to himself an ethos, or ethical character, attractive to readers and calculated to inspire confidence and trust. The narrator of the novel who speaks in the first person, *in propria persona* readers are led to think, strikes me as being this sort of rhetorically contrived persona, the creation of a self calculated to contrast most radically with Vonnegut's Billy Pilgrim-self. In a sense the first-person narrator is too good to be true, too much an obvious embodiment of humaneness, pacificism, good will, and honesty to be taken as the real man. His speaking of himself as "an old fart with his memories and his Pall Malls" (p. 2), whose worst vice seems to be getting drunk and exercising the skills of telephone operators, is in part what I have in mind. Numerous other passages seem contrived to portray this Vonnegut as a really good guy trying to live his life peacefully and virtuously, incapable of a vicious thought or deed, and a devoted family man to boot. He is a Will Rogers, too, saying in effect, "I never met a man I didn't like," when he expresses his belief that "nobody was ridiculous or bad or disgusting" (p. 7).

The image Vonnegut projects of himself as a writer is of the same order: the image of a humble, self-deprecating hard worker with no pretensions about the quality of his work:

> I would hate to tell you what this lousy little book cost me in money and anxiety and time. (p. 2)

His promise to Mary O'Hare contributes to this image—"I don't think this book of mine is ever going to be finished..."—and also sounds a note of moral herosim—"I'll call it 'The Children's Crusade'" (p. 13)—a note amplified in his comment on Lot's wife:

> But she did look back, and I love her for that because it was so human....
> This one is a failure, and had to be, since it was written by a pillar of salt. (p. 19)

Every word may be perfectly sincere, yet I must entertain the theory that this self-characterization is still a *persona, not a revelation of the whole man*, precisely because in no way does this Vonnegut recognize or embrace his Billy Pilgrim-self who would welcome release from the world of familial, professional, and moral responsibility.

The satirist that I have earlier shown at work is the satirist self or voice of this persona of Vonnegut, the skeptical, subtly critical, and admirably skilled satirist who in unobtrusive ways exposes and ridicules the deficiencies and absurdities of Billy Pilgrim's Tralfamadorianism, attacking the deterministic nihilism that his responsible moral character finds deplorable. He is a moderately optimistic realist and humanist, determined to fight to preserve the humane values he represents; his sober awareness of the possibility of failure will not deter him from trying to counter a philosophy that would reduce man to a machine.

The other satirical self is no less a persona of Vonnegut, despite his appearance in the novel in the character and science fiction of Kilgore Trout. Trout is a projection of Vonnegut's pessimistic self, the cynic in Vonnegut. Trout's voice is the satirical voice of Vonnegut's Billy Pilgrim-self. Trout is "a bitter man" (p. 142) whose science fiction embodies nothing but contempt for humanity, despair over the human lot, and the frustration of living in an absurd universe. The Trout of *Slaughterhouse-Five* differs radically from the Trout of *God Bless You, Mr. Rosewater*. This Trout has no tinge of that Trout's benevolence and optimism, none of his anguished desire to alleviate suffering, none of his hope that "hatred of useless human beings and the cruelties we inflict upon them for their own good need not be parts of human nature."[10] The Trout of *Slaughterhouse-Five* is obsessed with the despicableness of humanity and expresses unalleviated scorn for the world.

This is the science-fiction writer whose cynicism Billy Pilgrim has imbibed in reading dozens of his books: he is responsible for teaching Billy that the world is not worth one's concern. Billy, as has been seen, has been taught effectively by Trout, or rather by the man who created Kilgore Trout, by the pessimistic self of Vonnegut who has invested in Trout his own darkest vision of life. The cynic in Vonnegut wrote the novels of Kilgore Trout, reflecting in them a savagely pessimistic, cynical view that is in direct opposition to the moderately optimistic humanism of the other satirist.

The tension generated by the conflict of these opposing satirical voices, corresponding as it does to the tension generated by the conflict between the divided selves of the novelist, illustrates how masterfully Vonnegut has controlled every component of the novel. The satirical dimensions of the novel fuse with the narrative mode and structure to give *Slaughterhouse-Five* a total organic form and thus a total impact greater than Vonnegut had achieved in his earlier novels. A description of its organic form will show why I place Vonnegut among the masters of contemporary satiric fiction.

EXPERIENCING THE HUMAN PREDICAMENT

The term needed to describe the form of *Slaughterhouse-Five* is *dynamic tension*, a term and a concept appearing in *Cat's Cradle*; and the novels in which one can trace Vonnegut's developing artistic maturity and accomplishment are *Cat's Cradle* and *God Bless You, Mr. Rosewater*. Both are powerfully effective novels, and I intend no adverse criticism when I suggest that in them I can detect the rudiments of an aesthetic principle that Vonnegut has mastered in the writing of *Slaughterhouse-Five*.

In *Cat's Cradle*, dynamic tension exists exclusively as a concept in the content of the novel rather than functions as a principle of its form. The narrator John encounters Bokonon's theory of "Dynamic Tension" in Philip Castle's book about San Lorenzo and defines the theory as Bokonon's "sense of a priceless equilibrium between good and evil." John adds, "It was the belief of Bokonon that good societies could be built only by pitting good against evil, and by keeping the tension between the two high at all times."[11] The theory has been put into practice on San Lorenzo in the opposition between Papa Monzano and Bokonon, and John realizes that the practice will have to continue when he becomes president since he can provide for the people only the "entertainment" they derive from the conflict of good and evil.

In form, *Cat's Cradle* traces from his point of view the development of the narrator, largely an education in Bokononism, culminating in an implied act of discipleship to Bokonon. He is the younger man who, having already written his history of human stupidity, will do as Bokonon would do were he younger—climb the mountain to die, "grinning horribly, and thumbing [his] nose at You Know Who."[12] The reader's intellect is exercised considerably in reflection on the nature of good and evil, on religion and illusion, and on the stupidity of man, but the form does not realize a tension of its own. The first-person narration rather straightforwardly traces events as they unfold. "Dynamic Tension" remains a concept that readers are told about.

But in *God Bless You, Mr. Rosewater*, though no explicit mention of dynamic tension appears, the concept has become an aesthetic principle controlling and ordering the complete content of the novel; and it very nearly succeeds in controlling the form. The novel does realize dynamic tension in its form, but the tension ultimately becomes an ideological opposition that engages the mind rather than a compelling equilibrium between opposing forces that engages the emotions.

Abstractly speaking, *God Bless You, Mr. Rosewater* succeeds in creating a bipolar conflict between opposed psychic realities that draw an almost equal response from the reader. One pole can be called *rapaciousness*, deep seated in the human psyche. Samaritrophia, "hysterical indifference to the troubles of those less fortunate than oneself" (p. 41), permits rapaciousness to flourish. Senator Rosewater is the theorist who articulates the philosophy of rapaciousness, with assistance from Thurmond McAllister; Norman Mushari is its prime practitioner; and Lila Buntline as child prodigy gives promise that rapaciousness will have a prosperous future. The speech and behavior of these and other characters is reinforced by numerous passages calculated to depict rapaciousness as a reality in the American psyche and way of life, shared in various degrees by all Americans: Eliot's history of the Rosewater family and his description of the Money River, the Senator's speech on the Golden Age, the antisocialist pamphlet McAllister sent to Stewart Buntline, and the orphanage oath. All these and more, though satirically heightened, project a realistic awareness of the force of rapaciousness as manifested in American life. It can be called *enlightened self-interest* and it does have more than just an aura of respectability, so thoroughly is it ingrained in the economic and social system. But fundamentally it is greed, and Vonnegut forces one to face the truth: greed is a reality of human nature.

The other pole, ostensibly equal in power and reality to rapaciousness, is *humanitarianism*, love of one's fellow human beings and a selfless urge to help "those less fortunate than oneself." In its highest form, humanitarianism is agapé, and Eliot Rosewater is both its theorist and practitioner. The plight of characters like Diana Moon Glampers, Stella Wakeby, Roland Barry, and Selena Deal impresses upon one an inescapable reality of American life: the misery of the unloved masses. The selfless altruism of human nature is evoked by their plight.

The form of the novel forces one to contemplate one's own divided self. One is compelled to admit that rapaciousness and samaritrophia are normal, so normal that one has to agree with the rapacious characters who think Eliot crazy for devoting his life to unloved and unlovable, useless people. But one is also compelled to agree that the "insane" behavior of Eliot does fulfill the very real needs of people whose plight arouses one's compassion and calls upon one's own selflessness. One is drawn between the two poles.

The tension is real, but it is not dynamic: the satirist in Vonnegut allows an easy resolution to the tension. Rapaciousness is portrayed in such morally repugnant, satirically exaggerated terms that, though one recognizes the stuff of truth in it and intellectually admits to its being a pole of his own nature, one can not be drawn to it by powerful psychic urges. And the satire directed against Eliot for playing God likewise distances one emotionally from selflessness. Though it is compassionate satire and readers sympathize with Eliot's attempt to give uncritical godlike love to people who desperately need it, the ultimate effect of the satire is to portray humanitarianism as an agapé impossible of human attainment. The satire undercuts a potentially deep psychic response. The novel leaves readers not in a state of emotional conflict and crisis, pulled between opposing psychic forces, but in a state of intellectual detachment, comfortably disengaged, thinking about an ideological opposition that they know rather than feel can not be resolved.

One need consider only one pole of the tension created in *Slaughterhouse-Five* to understand why it is truly a dynamic tension, why it precludes distancing and allows no intellectual detachment, and why it appeals to the deepest psychic urges. Deterministic nihilism, the Tralfamadorian philosophy, is that one pole in tension with humanism. Deterministic nihilism exercises a compelling attraction because it has the force of apparently irrefutable truth: it codifies in simple yet profound form the belief of contemporary man that the universe he is forced to inhabit is meaningless and purposeless, as is his life. All of the tenets of determinism reflect truths of his existence that he can not escape; and they lead inexorably, it seems, with the force of flawless logic, to nihilism.

And that logic speaks directly to the unconscious, releasing psychic urges that may ultimately prove impossible to contain. Who has not felt himself the victim of enormous forces that he knows he can not control? Who has not concluded that his life is predetermined since events occur for which he can find no rational explanation and isolate no responsible agent? Who does not agonize over his inability to comprehend not only cosmic forces but also identifiable global and even local operations of, say, politics and economics, not to speak of the human behavior he personally observes every day? Who has read history and seen history in the making without being overwhelmed by the stupidity, cruelty, and barbarous inhumanity of man to man and without projecting the past and present into the infinite future? In the face of his own death, his obliteration, and the senseless slaughter of millions, who has not doubted the value of life itself?

The sensitive reader can not escape the observation that Billy Pilgrim has learned his deterministic nihilism from reliable observers of the universe, so perfectly does it seem to accord with reality. Reason seems to command the descent into a spiritual oubliette. But the psyche commands man with more power than does reason. To be able to say "So it goes," to want to believe that "Everything was beautiful, and nothing hurt," to be able to ignore the bad moments and look only at the good—are not these desires one's own psychic urges to realize the edenic paradise retained in the mythic unconscious? One can not remain detached. Billy's flight from an inhospitable universe draws one with him.

To this powerful attraction, the psyche can raise but one defense, one counterforce. And that one force creates the tension that makes of the novel the battleground of psychic conflict. The Tralfamadorians come close to suggesting the strength of this counterforce when they say "that every creature and plant in the Universe is a machine. It amuses them that so many Earthlings are offended by the idea of being machines" (p. 133). Offended? The word is too mild. "Earthlings" rebel against the idea from the depths of their psyches. For better or for worse, "Earthlings" are human *beings*, and they know that to capitulate to deterministic nihilism is to become a machine, to enter into a death-in-life, because it deprives man of his essence. This humanistic commitment to life is what the novel has made readers feel as deeply as they feel the attraction of deterministic nihilism; it engages readers because Vonnegut feels it himself, just as he feels, like all men, the attraction of death-in-life. Because of Dresden and Vietnam, Vonnegut had to dance with death, and the dance restored his commitment to life, to the value of the individual human life, his own and that of every other human being. Life against death-in-life—that is the psychic conflict at the very core of the novel.

Vonnegut has succeeded in realizing the full potential of dynamic tension as an aesthetic principle because within himself he has realized its potency as a psychic conflict. *Slaughterhouse-Five* drives deeply into the human condition and elicits profound responses because its art is a projection of his own psychic tension, of his own divided self. In a brilliantly imaginative act, by projecting his nihilistic self in the character of Billy Pilgrim and his humanistic self in the first-person narrator, Vonnegut has faced the truth of his own being. The struggle goes on, must go on, for there is no release. Only a tenuous hold on life preserves him from death-in-life. His readers know it, too: Vonnegut forces them to see themselves in the same predicament. To experience *Slaughterhouse-Five* is to experience the human predicament.

NOTES

1. Kurt Vonnegut, Jr., *Slaughterhouse-Five* (New York: Dell Publishing Co., 1969), p. 52. Further page references to this Delta edition will be given in parentheses in the text.
2. Jerome Klinkowitz and John Somer, eds., *The Vonnegut Statement* (New York: Dell Publishing Co., 1973), p. 3.
3. John Somer, "Geodesic Vonnegut; Or, If Buckminster Fuller Wrote Novels," in *The Vonnegut Statement*, p. 230.
4. Somer, pp. 244-46.
5. A discrepancy here must be recognized. On p. 142, the date of 1964 is made explicit and precise: "Billy met [Trout] for the first time in 1964"; at that meeting Billy invited Trout to his anniversary party "only two days hence." Yet, on p. 146, the party to which Billy invited Trout is identified as his *eighteenth* wedding anniversary; and on p. 151 the age of Billy's son Robert is given as seventeen. Since Billy and Valencia were married and Robert was conceived in 1948, six months after he left the veterans' hospital (p. 102), where he had himself committed in the springtime of 1948 (p. 86), the date should be 1966. Though I reject out of hand a seminar student's waggish excuse that husbands can never remember anniversaries, I have no other explanation of the discrepancy. Whether I argue logically that the exception *tests* the validity of the rule or illogically that it *proves* the rule, the fact is that the date 1964 is there for everyone to see. Given the dominance of structural patterns that force the reader to

associate various widely separated details of the novel, I have no recourse but to assume that the explicit date 1964 is cited for the purpose I have given.

Other discrepancies, inconsequential as far as I can see, should also be noted. First, p. 21, in reference to the plane crash, the text reads, "Everybody was killed but Billy"; on p. 134, "Everybody was killed but Billy and the copilot." Second, on p. 38, Billy's age in 1965 is given as forty-one. Since he was born in 1922, he could not be that age in 1965. And finally on p. 133, the line, "Billy Pilgrim got onto a chartered airplane in Ilium twenty-five years after that," should read "twenty-*three* years," since "that" refers to Billy's arrival at Slaughterhouse-Five in January of 1945. The chartered plane crashed "early in 1968" (p. 21).

6. As I shall later explain, it is misleading to refer to Billy's escape to Tralfamadore in 1967 since he did not even conceive of Tralfamadore until after the plane crash in 1968. More exactly, in 1968 he locates his imaginary escape to Tralfamadore on his daughter's wedding night in 1967. Psychologically speaking, he does so because he realizes that in 1967 he was dead to this world. In 1967 he had fallen asleep at his work and could not remember his age or the year. He had found himself weeping for no apparent reason. Narratively, Vonnegut frames between the sleeping and the weeping the scene at the Lions Club where the Marine Major advocated bombing North Vietnam back into the Stone Age and Billy was himself a stone: he was not moved to protest the bombing. He had lost interest in his profession and had no reaction to the social crises of Ilium: in the ghetto wrecked in a riot, Billy had ignored the black who wanted to talk to him. In 1967 Billy had in effect abandoned humanity and this world; in other words, though he had not yet invented Tralfamadore, he had "traveled" far from Earth and his human responsibilities.

7. Somer, pp. 243-44: "some readers must find consolation in the third short paragraph of Billy's story: 'He says.' ...It seems to imply that the narrator is dubious of Billy's story and that the reader should be also . . . . But that implication is simply not valid."

8. I have quoted the second intrusion. The first intrusion, p. 58, is a simple exclamation: "I was there. So was my old war buddy, Bernard V. O'Hare." The third appears on p. 129. The fourth, p. 184, somewhat like the second, introduces the author into the story as a character whose actions are recorded in the first-person plural rather than the third person: "I was there. O'Hare was there. We had spent the past two nights in the blind innkeeper's stable."

9. They are also associated by the fact that each has as a souvenir a ceremonial Luftwaffe saber (p. 5 and pp. 168-69). These direct associations are limited to the war experiences.

10. (New York: Dell Publishing Co., 1965), p. 187.

11. (New York: Dell Publishing Co., 1963), p. 74.

12. *Cat's Cradle*, p. 127.

WORKS CITED

Barth, John. *Giles Boat-Boy; or The Revised New Syllabus*. Garden City, New York: Doubleday and Company,1966.

———. *Giles Goat-Boy; or The Revised New Syllabus*. Greenwich, Connecticut: Fawcett Publications, Inc., n.d.

Burgess, Anthony. *A Clockwork Orange*. London: William Heinemann, Ltd., 1962.

———. *A Clockwork Orange*. New York: W. W. Norton and Company, Inc., 1963.

Campbell, Joseph. *Myths to Live By*. New York: The Viking Press, 1972.

Klinkowitz, Jerome, and Somer, John, eds. *The Vonnegut Statement*. New York: Dell Publishing Co., 1973.

Meras, Phyllis. "John Barth: A Truffle No Longer." New York *Times*, 7 August 1966, Section 7, p. 22.

Morris, Robert K. *The Consolations of Ambiguity*. Columbia, Missouri: University of Missouri Press, 1971.

Murdoch, Iris. "Against Dryness." *Encounter*, 16 (January 1961): 16–20.

Scholes, Robert. *The Fabulators*. New York: Oxford University Press, 1967.

Time, 11 April 1969, p. 106.

Vonnegut, Kurt, Jr. *Cat's Cradle*. New York: Holt, Rinehart, and Winston, Inc.; Dell Publishing Co., 1963.

———. *God Bless You, Mr. Rosewater: or, Pearls Before Swine*. New York: Holt, Rinehart, and Winston, Inc.; Dell Publishing Co., 1965.

———. *Slaughterhouse-Five, or The Children's Crusade*. New York: Delacorte Press/Seymour Lawrence; Dell Publishing Co., 1969.

The Major Fiction
of Burgess, Barth, and Vonnegut

Anthony Burgess

The Doctor Is Sick. London: William Heinemann, Ltd., 1960.

The Right to an Answer. London: William Heinemann, Ltd., 1960; New York: W. W. Norton and Company, Inc., 1962.

Devil of a State. London: William Heinemann, Ltd., 1961; New York: W. W. Norton and Company, Inc. 1962.

One Hand Clapping. London: Peter Davis, 1961; New York: Alfred A. Knopf, Inc., 1972. (First published under name of Joseph Kell.)

The Worm and the Ring. London: William Heinemann, Ltd., 1961.

A Clockwork Orange. London: William Heinemann, Ltd., 1962; New York: W. W. Norton and Company, Inc., 1963.

The Wanting Seed. London: William Heinemann, Ltd., 1962; New York: W. W. Norton and Company, Inc., 1963.

Honey for the Bears. London: William Heinemann, Ltd., 1963; New York: W. W. Norton and Company, Inc., 1964.

The Eve of St. Venus. London: Sedgewick and Jackson, 1964; New York: W. W. Norton and Company, Inc., 1970.

A Long Day Wanes: A Malayan Trilogy. New York: W. W. Norton and Company, Inc., 1964.

A Vision of Battlements. London: Sedgewick and Jackson, 1965; New York: W. W. Norton and Company, Inc., 1966.

Tremor of Intent. London: William Heinemann, Ltd., 1966; New York: W. W. Norton and Company, Inc., 1966.

Enderby. New York: W. W. Norton and Company, Inc., 1968.

M.F. London: Jonathan Cape, 1971; New York: Alfred A. Knopf, Inc., 1971.

Napoleon Symphony. New York: Alfred A. Knopf, Inc., 1974.

The Clockwork Testament or Enderby's End. New York: Alfred A. Knopf, Inc., 1975.

John Barth

The Floating Opera. New York: Appleton-Century-Crofts, 1956;

The Floating Opera. Revised edition. Garden City, New York: Doubleday and Company, 1967.

End of the Road. Garden City, New York: Doubleday and Company, 1958;

End of the Road. Revised edition. Garden City, New York: Doubleday and Company, 1967.

The Sot-Weed Factor. Garden City, New York: Doubleday and Company, 1960;

The Sot-Weed Factor. Revised edition. Garden City, New York: Doubleday and Company, 1967.

Giles Goat-Boy; or The Revised New Syllabus. Garden City, New York: Doubleday and Company, 1966.

Lost in the Funhouse; Fiction for Print, Tape, Live Voice. Garden City, New York: Doubleday and Company, 1968.

Chimera. New York: Random House, Inc., 1972.

Kurt Vonnegut, Jr.

Player Piano. New York: Charles Scribner's Sons, 1952.

The Sirens of Titan. New York: Dell Publishing Co., 1959.

Mother Night. New York: Fawcett Publications, Inc., 1961.

Cat's Cradle. New York: Holt, Rinehart, and Winston, Inc., 1963.

God Bless You, Mr. Rosewater: or, Pearls Before Swine. New York: Holt, Rinehart, and Winston, Inc., 1965.

Slaughterhouse-Five, or The Children's Crusade. New York: Delacorte Press/Seymour Lawrence, 1969.

Breakfast of Champions, or Goodbye, Blue Monday. Delacorte Press/Seymour Lawrence, 1973.

Index